AMERICA
RETURN TO GOD

REPENT FROM SIN ★
REBUILD THE WALL ★
REPAIR THE GATES ★
RESTORE THE DREAM ★

A Message to 21st Century America
From the Books of Ezra,
Nehemiah and Esther

To John + Marcia,
Alveda C. King

By Evangelist Alveda C. King

Foreword by Pastor Mike Berry
Afterward by Bishop Vincent Matthews

America Return to God: Repent from Sin, Rebuild the Wall,
Repair the Gates, Restore the Dream
© 2016 – Alveda C. King
All rights reserved.

Unless otherwise identified, Scripture quotations are from the HOLY
BIBLE, English Standard Version, King James Version, Lexham English
Bible, The Message, Modern English Version, New Kings James Version,
New Living Translation, World English Bible, Copyright © 1973, 1978,
1984, by International Bible Society. Used by permission of Zondervan
Publishing House.

Please note that Elijah List Publication's publishing style capitalizes
certain pronouns in Scripture that refer to the Father, Son, and Holy Spirit,
and may differ from some publishers' styles.

ELIJAH LIST PUBLICATIONS
528 Ellsworth St. SW, Albany, OR 97321 USA

*"The lion has roared—who will not fear? The Sovereign Lord has spoken—who can
but prophesy?"* Amos 3:8

This book and all other Elijah List Publications products and resources are
available online at our webstore at www.elijahshopper.com.

For more information, call us at 541-926-3250 or 866-354-5245 or send us an
email at: info@elijahlist.net. Or reach us on the Internet: www.elijahlist.com.

ISBN 978-1-938311-35-2 / Library of Congress Control Number: 2016960494
Printed in the United States. For Worldwide Distribution.
1 2 3 4 5 6 7 8 9 10 11 / 12 01 16

Managing Editor: Julie A. Smith
Editors: Julie A. Smith and Teresa Kephart
Cover Design: Jenn Loewen

DEDICATION

With gratitude, I dedicate this book to God—Father, Son and Holy Spirit.

With deep appreciation, I thank God for my natural family, my church family, my friends, and co-laborers for Christ.

I especially appreciate the support and love extended from The Elijah List in editing and publishing this book.

Dear readers, may God bless each of you as we share in God's goodness, which I have labored to bring to you in this book.

ENDORSEMENTS

Watching history play out is amazing! Dr. Martin Luther King Jr. probably never foresaw a major part of his legacy would include his niece Dr. Alveda King, who now carries a great torch for the King Family and for the LORD Himself.

The Word says, "Blessed are the peacemakers for THEY will inherit the earth." Alveda King in "AMERICA RETURN TO GOD" is a peacemaker of epic proportions and uses her prophetic gifting along with her now-celebrity status (you've seen her on *Fox News* many times) to call America and to call all the races back to God and to call the Church back to its first love.

In this book, Dr. Alveda King cries out, as it were, with a loud voice, "It's the season for the Hidden Prophets to Speak out!"

You need to get this book for yourself and for your church! And while you're at it, buy one for a friend!

Steve Shultz, Founder and President
ELIJAH LIST PUBLICATIONS, Inc.

Alveda King is one of the bravest women I know. She is one of the voices in America that we need to pay careful attention to in this critical hour. I love her and I am proud to call her my friend.

For some of us who are from the white community, we need to read this book! It might be hard for a few as I know the mention of the words "white privilege" either hurts you or makes you mad. However, Alveda explains to us the "why" of this term and we need to learn from her.

We cannot say that we the people, whatever our ethnicity, want to heal the United States without taking time to read this thoughtful book. It is strong medicine to heal a broken nation and we need it to become one.

Cindy Jacobs, Cofounder
Generals International

The timing of Alveda King's book is impeccable—as we NOW have the opportunity to "Return to God" and heal our land. Alveda does not shy away from tough subjects we are dealing with in our culture today and offers a clarion call to repent and rebuild our nation. There are strategic keys Alveda offers to us along with a message of *hope, oneness* and *unity in spirit* among the brethren. God is telling His Church to come together as one and take authority over our land. The prophetic decree that Alveda boldly offers us in this hour: "America Return to God!"

Dr. Jim Garlow
Senior Pastor, Skyline Church

Martin Luther King, Jr., spoke to America about a dream. His niece, Alveda King, shows us in this book how to keep pursuing it.

Fr. Frank Pavone
National Director, Priests for Life

My beloved friend, Alveda King, is a child of the King. Her biological fathers are kings. Her spiritual Father is the King of kings. She is indeed a king in every sense, and also a new covenant priest anointed to see and declare with prophetic authority in our nation and at this time. I strongly encourage you to assimilate the spirit of hope and purpose that is so skillfully prescribed in this exemplary book, *America Return to God*. Alveda King is uniquely and divinely designed, conceived, and assigned to be a force for social justice and healing. This "seer" becomes our guide in this book to show us the way to do our part "to repair the gates, rebuild the wall, restore the dream, and RETURN TO GOD!"

Pastor Frank Amedia
Touch Heaven Ministries

There is no more seasoned voice to call our nation back to God than Alveda King. Many forget that Dr. Martin Luther King carried a transformative message of Christian love and repentance. This was at the core of his ministry. She carries that same mantle as a birthright. The passion and fire of her forefathers' flows in her spirit. Therefore, your heart will be "strangely warmed" as you read the pages of this book. God still has a dream for America. He still has a safe harbor for our families and a specific calling for each of us to enter in the flow of the next Great Awakening.

Bishop Harry Jackson
Senior Pastor, Hope Christian Church

God is up to something and we each have a role to play together in His divine plan. In this powerful book, Dr. Alveda King shows from the Bible how America can and must return to God. Drawing on God's word and insights from her own inspiring family heritage, Dr. Alveda King points the way forward! Powerful, riveting, inspiring, insightful and perfect for our times! I highly recommend it!

Dick Bott
Founder and Chairman, Bott Radio Network

TABLE OF CONTENTS

SCRIPTURE THEME

"From the days of your fathers you have gone away from My ordinances and have not kept them. Return to Me, and I will return to you, says the LORD of Hosts. But you say, 'How shall we return?'" (Malachi 3:7 MEV)

"If My people, who are called by My name, will humble themselves and pray, and seek My face and turn from their wicked ways, then I will hear from Heaven, and will forgive their sin and will heal their land." (2 Chronicles 7:14 MEV)

"Please remember the word that You commanded Your servant Moses, saying, 'If you behave unfaithfully, then I will scatter you among the nations, but if you return to Me and keep My commandments and do them, though your outcasts are under the farthest part of the heavens, I will gather them from there and bring them back to the place where I have chosen to establish My name.' Now these are Your servants and Your people, whom You have redeemed by Your great power and by Your strong hand." (Nehemiah 1:8-10 MEV)

"Then Jesus said to them, 'Truly, truly I say to you, the Son can do nothing of Himself, but what He sees the Father do. For whatever He does, likewise the Son does.'" (John 5:19 MEV)

*"…The time is fulfilled, and the kingdom of God is at hand. Repent
and believe the gospel."*
(Mark 1:15 MEV)

*"Why are the nations so angry? Why do they waste their time with
futile plans? The kings of the earth prepare for battle; the rulers plot
together against the LORD and against his anointed one. 'Let us
break their chains,' they cry, 'and free ourselves from slavery to God.'
But the one who rules in heaven laughs. The Lord scoffs at them.
Then in anger he rebukes them, terrifying them with his fierce fury.
For the Lord declares, 'I have placed my chosen king on the throne in
Jerusalem, on my holy mountain.' The king proclaims the LORD's
decree: 'The LORD said to me, "You are my son. Today I have
become your Father. Only ask, and I will give you the nations as your
inheritance, the whole earth as your possession. You will break them
with an iron rod and smash them like clay pots."' Now then, you
kings, act wisely! Be warned, you rulers of the earth! Serve the
LORD with reverent fear, and rejoice with trembling. Submit to
God's royal son, or he will become angry, and you will be destroyed in
the midst of all your activities—for his anger flares up in an instant.
But what joy for all who take refuge in him!" (Psalms 2:1-12 NLT)*

*"And now abide faith, hope and love. The greatest
of these is Love… Love never fails."*
(I Corinthians 13:13)

*"Of one blood, God made all people to live together
on the earth." (Acts 17:26)*

Then Jesus said to the disciples, "Have faith in God. I tell you the truth, you can say to this mountain, 'May you be lifted up and thrown into the sea,' and it will happen. But you must really believe it will happen and have no doubt in your heart. I tell you, you can pray for anything, and if you believe that you've received it, it will be yours. But when you are praying, first forgive anyone you are holding a grudge against, so that your Father in heaven will forgive your sins, too."
(Mark 11:22-26)

"For in Christ Jesus neither circumcision nor uncircumcision means anything, but faith which works through love". (Galatians 5:6 MEV)

FOREWORD
By Pastor Mike Berry

Evangelist Alveda King's book is a prophetic call for us to actively embrace the work of rebuilding the infrastructures of our nation to meet the needs of future generations. It's a call to end the devaluation of life and end the culture of death that looms across our nation. Evangelist King's book is a call to America to repent, repair, rebuild, restore, and lead the world in returning to God just as her forefathers, Granddaddy Martin Luther King, Sr., her natural father Alfred Daniel Williams (A.D.) King, and her uncle Dr. Martin Luther (M.L.) King, Jr. did in their lifetimes.

Using the Books of Ezra, Nehemiah, Esther, and several Bible passages together as a focus piece to her message, Evangelist King's timely piece shows us the way in which every family and every individual within the Body of Christ can fulfill the generational responsibilities given to them.

In the 21st century, America is in the crosshairs of global flux, while standing at a major crossroad in our history. Jeremiah 6:16 (ESV) seems to resonate with many of us today. "Thus says the Lord: Stand by the roads, and look, and ask for the ancient paths, where the good way is; and walk in it, and find rest for your souls. But they said, 'We will not walk in it.'"

As a result, the Hebrew people were carried off into captivity, lost their land, and found themselves unable to sing the Lord's song in a strange land (see Psalm 137:4). The whole book of Lamentations is a dire warning to God's people that if we refuse to do what God has asked us to do we will face the dire consequences of our poor decisions.

Since our beginning, our nation's history has been entangled with foundations of dehumanization, slavery, racism, genocide, and injustice. However, God has been calling all of us to a place of healing, reconciliation, and restoration. The Bill of

Rights, The US Constitution, and Dr. Martin Luther King's prophetic "I Have a Dream" speech have served as God's prophetic call to become the people God intended for us to be. God's vision was for a nation "to be a city on a hill" that exemplifies what it means to be the people of God.

Even though many godly people have been instrumental down through our history in addressing the injustices of their time and generations, God is now calling and still waiting for the Body of Christ to lead the way out of our national sins and bondage here in the 21st century. However, like ancient Israel who ignored the prophet Jeremiah's voice, we now stand in a new time, with a new generation, at the same crossroads and face the possible loss of everything our forefathers have worked to establish a world for us to enjoy.

While it would be counterproductive to fault them for what they refused or were unable to see and do, we have an obligation to make it clear that injustices remaining from the past and those present can and must be corrected here on our watch! Matthew 13:25 states, "But while men slept, his enemy came and sowed tares among the wheat, and he went his way." We can only address the injustices that stand before us in our time.

None of us is exempt from the responsibility of stewarding what God has given to us to do. While some things are different today than they have been in the past, the job is not yet finished. Thus the question remains, "Why has it been so difficult for us to embrace and consistently live out Dr. Martin Luther King's dream?"

The Holy Spirit's call on the Body of Christ for the last 50 years has been Isaiah 58:12, "Those from among you shall build the old waste places; You shall raise up the foundations of many generations; And you shall be called the Repairer of the Breach, the Restorer of Streets to Dwell In."

It's amazing to me today, in light of everything that has happened, that we don't yet collectively recognize the prophetic view of God in anointing an Iraqi man named Abram, renaming him as *Abraham*, thus prophetically connecting the sons of Noah—Ham, Shem and Japheth; thus defining the future generations of Jews, Africans and Gentiles together as "redeemable humanity." Now what remains is that Abraham's sons, Ishmael and Isaac, also be reconciled under the new covenant—the agape love of God. That ancient battle which started between a father, Abraham, his two wives, Sarah and Hagar, and their sons Ishmael and Isaac can be resolved—if only we understand that agape love will heal the wounds of rejection and rebellion that allows the battle to continue.

In Acts 17:26 the Bible explains to us that: "God has given all of us seasons of the year and boundaries to work within." Just as God assigned individual families to repair the Gates in Nehemiah's time, Evangelist Alveda King so passionately calls on each of us to "get involved in God's work" and lay the foundation for our children's futures instead of destroying their futures.

We only have so much time. We don't have to take on the whole world; we just have to work within the spheres of influence God has given to each of us.

"Human progress is neither automatic nor inevitable. Even a superficial look at history reveals that no social advance rolls in on the wheel's inevitability. Every step towards the goal of justice requires sacrifice, suffering, and struggle; the tireless exertions and passionate concern of dedicated individuals.

"Without persistent effort, time itself becomes an ally of the insurgent and primitive forces of irrational emotionalism and social destruction. This is no time for apathy or complacency. This is a time for vigorous and positive action." - Dr. Martin Luther King, Jr.

This book gives us a blueprint for Bible-based social justice, a path to healing America's wounds. I highly recommend you take the time to read it and digest what God is calling you to do today!

Rev. Mike Berry
President & CEO
Justice United, Inc.
Annapolis, Maryland

INTRODUCTION

In the mid-1990's, God moved on my heart to do a Bible Study about Queen Esther. From there, God used Queen Esther's testimony to call me into full-time ministry. Oh, it took a few years for me to get here, but the journey has been memorable.

> *"For if indeed you keep silent at this time, relief and deliverance will arise for the Jews from another place, and you and the family of your father will perish. Who knows? Perhaps you have come to a royal position for a time such as this." (Esther 4:13-14 LEB)*

Do you recognize the correlation among the passages? The enemy is forever at the gates. It is always up to the believers to trust God and resist the enemy. It's also interesting to note that the two queens in the book of Esther, Vashti and Esther, were dealing with the same man. The king had a brash side—a reckless side. He wanted to parade his beautiful wife before his inebriated friends. Vashti chose the emotional response—she was offended and refused to obey her husband. On the other hand, Esther chose prayer, fasting and humility, and was able to turn away his wrath with a soft approach.

In the 21st century, we are facing brash heads of state, political candidates, and all sorts of leaders who need prayer. Are we more likely to take offense as Vashti did? Or will we seek the higher frequency of prayer that Esther favored? The issues we are facing today are far too serious to be handled by offense and emotions. There is a lesson to be learned here. Herein also is the acknowledgment of my call into ministry.

Often, people will ask: "How were you called into ministry?" My "call" came out of the book of Esther in the Bible; but before I explain how, please let me lay a foundation.

In retrospect, whenever I consider the answer regarding my "calling" I am generally reminded of the many Bible accounts of how people were called to serve the Lord. I also think about how my human biological father, Rev. Alfred Daniel Williams King, was called at home in his kitchen.

In the early 1950s, my mother, Naomi Ruth Barber King, said that Daddy was walking and talking to someone "invisible" that she couldn't hear. She could and did hear Daddy saying things like, "I hear you Lord. What do You want me to do?"

Mother called my granddaddy, Dr. Martin Luther King, Sr., and asked him: "Dad, something is wrong with A. D. He is talking to himself, and I can't get him to stop. He is too agitated to hear me! What should I do?"

Mother explained what Daddy was saying, and what "whoever" he was talking to while seemingly alone in their bedroom seemed to be telling Daddy. Mother said that Granddaddy laughed and said: "Oh, don't worry baby. He's just getting the call."

Needless to say, Mother didn't quite understand all that was going on, but she was married into a family of preachers, and she had indeed heard of "the call." She trusted Granddaddy, and just waited until Daddy calmed down. The last thing Daddy said before sitting down and falling asleep was: "Okay Lord. I'll preach."

Please understand that Daddy's submission was not too easy. He had been running from the Lord most of his young life.

Daddy wanted to be a successful businessman and make a lot of money to support his family. God changed all of that.

(Photo from in 1963, King family legacy)

(You can learn more about my daddy at www.adkingfoundation.com; all about how he pastored churches, helped my uncle M. L. [Dr. Martin Luther King, Jr.] in the 20th Century Civil Rights Movement; and you will understand why he is one of my best mentors and one of my greatest human heroes.)

Uncle M. L. was also called to serve God at home at his kitchen table. As brothers, because of their fiery preaching styles, Uncle M. L. and Daddy were known as "the sons of thunder" during their lifetimes.

You can also learn about Uncle M. L.'s call to ministry in the book *A KNOCK AT MIDNIGHT*. Because "many are called, and few are chosen," some people are called by God to preach the Gospel. Actually, we are all called to be evangelists. Yet, everyone doesn't answer God when He calls us. Some people even go so far as to call themselves into ministry, without having heard from God. Even fewer of us obey God's call when it does come.

Some familiar ministry calls from the Bible include these: David was called in from the fields while keeping the sheep. Elisha was called by having Elijah throw his cloak over him while walking down the road. Jesus called the twelve to follow Him.

We also know how Esther, the queen, was called into service to be a vessel of deliverance for her people the Jews. The Book of Esther was always a favorite testimony for me, but I never expected for God to use Esther's life and ministry to call me to higher and deeper service.

I had been "saved" and water baptized in 1956, just five years after my birth on January 22, 1951. At five years of age, when Daddy and Granddaddy preached about Jesus, having been born of the Virgin Mary, having died on the cross and rose again, I believed that, and was baptized. Yet, it took nearly three decades, into 1983, for me to become "born again."

In 1983, it was after a compassionate hour in which a woman who was a coworker and used the Scriptures to enlighten me that I was a "sinner in need of grace." I learned from the Bible that day that indeed Jesus was born of the Virgin Mary; lived and ministered in the earth; died on the cross at Calvary, and shed His pure blood for my sins; went into Hell and defeated my enemy Satan; rose again on the third day, and is now seated on the throne in Heaven as my High Priest. I learned that Jesus is the Son of God and that God the Father, God the Son, and God the Holy Spirit loves me. Glory!

Well, from 1983 till about 1995, I began to confess my sins, tithe, and generally serve God the best I knew how. I joined Believers' Bible Christian Church in 1988, and have remained there for my spiritual covering. I was content with my life and wasn't looking for anything new to do. In fact, I had been ignoring various calls to join in ministry projects at the church, because I was "too busy" with other things.

Then, in 1995, I was at home in my "prayer room" on a Sunday morning. I had an "unction from the Holy Ghost" to read the entire book of Esther before I went to church that morning. Now, please understand that Sunday morning was a special quiet time for me. I had about an hour before I had to cook breakfast, feed and dress the children and myself, and still get to church on time. I can still remember that day, reading in my quiet room, with the presence of God making the world very beautiful in those moments. In my heart, I realized that God very likely wanted me to do something, and I didn't want my Father's house to be forgotten. I said a quick prayer and prepared to go to church.

I remember what happened at the altar call that morning during service almost as if it were yesterday. Pastor McNair spoke to the congregation, saying something like this: "If God is speaking to your heart this morning, if you know that God wants you to step up and serve Him because people are dying and need the Lord, then step out of your seat right now, and come around the altar."

I left the choir stand, and was on my feet and moving down to the altar. I remember falling on my face at the steps to the altar. Pastor walked back and forth across the platform, ministering. I remember his feet stopping just above my head, while I was sobbing, "Okay God." I guess I sounded like my daddy all those years ago.

Pastor McNair spoke these words: "Queen Esther, it is time for you to come off of your throne of complacency. There is a hole in the spirit in the city of Atlanta that needs to be filled."

Then, Pastor walked on and continued to minister. I knew God was speaking directly to me. I needed to do more for the Lord! I decided then, that whatever God wanted, I would do it. That was my "Queen Esther Moment," my "Esther Call."

Over the years, Pastor McNair would speak many prophetic words over my life. In the 1990's my pastor and mentor, Allen McNair, said to me: "You have an end-time ministry. You must prepare." Pastor gave me several books to read, and I began to explore the prophetic nature of ministry more deeply. During his lifetime, Pastor Allen McNair was an apostle, prophet, teacher and pastor. I have done my best to follow his Christian examples and teachings as he followed Christ our Savior.

During those earlier days at the BBCC ministry, Pastor McNair also prophesied that I would "stand before kings and leaders and proclaim the Gospel of the Lord." These words and more have become true in my life. He encouraged me to found "King for America" in 1995. Since that time, King for America has been founded and retired. My pro-life ministry with "Priests for Life" has been established, my father's memory is honored at www.adkingfoundation.com, I have participated in "Esther Call" conferences' across the land, and I have been blessed to share the Gospel of Jesus Christ with many and have seen souls won for Christ. It seems that I was truly born "for such a time as this."

At the beginning of the 21st Century, I watched America begin to crumble all around me. Early on, the horrors of 9/11 and the fall of the Twin Towers in Manhattan—along with the decline of our economy—were all a part of God's way of getting our attention, to help us see the need to return to Him, to truly become "One Nation under God."

Somehow, we as a nation missed the memo. What was needful was that we were to have returned to God, and He, according to 2 Chronicles 7:14, would forgive us, heal us, and rebuild our land. However, our nation followed our leaders and made the decree, "We will rebuild." There was very little repentance from America, and much blaming the terrorists for the decaying conditions of our world.

Somewhere along the way, I made the connection between the "rescue mission" of Queen Esther and the "restoration project" of Ezra and Nehemiah. Esther's compassion for her people, her humility and obedience to authority, and her fearless determination to stand up for justice simply resonated in my heart and life.

At the same time, I became increasingly aware that America was rapidly spiraling downhill in a catastrophic landslide. Again, the arrogance of the reaction to 9/11 was staggering, not springing from repentant hearts but rather from the pride of life, with proclamations of rebuilding from the strength of man, without sincerely calling on God to help.

Esthers, Daniels, Nehemiahs and Ezras—Arise!

At the end of the first decade of the 21st century, I began to read the Book of Esther. I simultaneously began a serious study of the books of Ezra and Nehemiah:

> *Ezra 8:22, "For I was ashamed to ask the king for a band of soldiers and horsemen to protect us against the enemy on our way, since we had told the king, 'The hand of our God is for good on all who seek him, and the power of his wrath is against all who forsake him.'"*

> *Nehemiah 1:3-4, "The remnant there in the province who had survived the exile is in great trouble and shame. The wall of Jerusalem is broken down, and its gates are destroyed by fire. As soon as I heard these words I sat down and wept and mourned for days, and I continued fasting and praying before the God of heaven."*

> *Nehemiah 2:8, "...for the good hand of my God was upon me."*

Daniel was in office the first year of King Cyrus' reign. Daniel and Esther fasted and prayed. Ezra and Nehemiah rebuilt the wall.

> *Ezra 5:13, "However, in the first year of Cyrus king of Babylon, Cyrus the king made a decree that this house of God should be rebuilt."*

> *Daniel 1:21, "And Daniel was there until the first year of King Cyrus."*

> *Daniel 6:28, "So this Daniel prospered during the reign of Darius and the reign of Cyrus the Persian."*

Ezra 1:8, "Cyrus king of Persia brought these out in the charge of Mithredath the treasurer, who counted them out to Sheshbazzar the prince of Judah."

During personal Bible study time, it came to me that we should be ashamed to say that we are trusting God, only to then turn to the world's solutions for our problems. I don't mean that we can't use what is available to use because the wealth of the wicked is laid up for the just. But do we trust that God will guide us in taking possession of the "spoils," or are we relying on getting the goods by our own strength?

For example, the early 21st century stimulus packages and freebies promised by our government may have had some "hidden treasures" in them; but as we rushed to receive the handouts, did we by faith rely on God to direct our approach for the solutions and supply our wants and needs? Or were we looking to God while using earthly solutions? I can't say that God will never instruct someone to do something that we, as Christians, would ordinarily not try because Peter had a dream to eat "unclean" food and God told him not to say what was clean or not, but to let God make those decisions. But do we come up with schemes on our own and then say that, "God blessed us," if we happen to win? I think not.

One reason that America borders on the brink of economic disaster and constant violent upheaval is that we have turned blind eyes and deaf ears to the plight of our brothers and sisters. Like Cain who killed his brother Abel, we have despised good and have turned away from caring about what happens to our brothers and sisters. We must humble ourselves as Nehemiah did: "When I heard these things, I sat down and wept. For some days, I mourned and fasted and prayed before the God of heaven" (Nehemiah 1:4 NIV).

Early in 2016, America found herself facing the choice of repenting first of her own sins, before taking on the ills of the world; or continuing along the troubled paths that have been set before us. Yes, repenting and returning to God, rebuilding the foundations of a nation that once tried to live up to the creed of being "One nation under God"; or forsaking God altogether and going the way of other civilizations that forsook God and perished. The saga of Sodom and Gomorrah is perhaps one of the more extreme examples of such, but we must ask ourselves if we are closer to experiencing a similar fate than we might realize.

Amazingly, in 2015, there emerged a least likely presidential candidate who wanted to "make America great again." He started speaking of "building a wall" around America's borders. The people became fearful, the naysayers became furious. Yet the talk of America's wall continued.

All of this talk about a "wall" for America has actually caused the hearts of America's prayer warriors to hope again, realizing that a wall must have a strong foundation, a sturdy rock, and a chief cornerstone. Finally, 21st century America seems to have taken notice that something more is required if there is truly to be hope for America.

Yes, there is hope, and there still may be time to return to God and rebuild God's wall of protection around our nation. If we sincerely desire to rebuild our nation, there is much to be learned from the lessons in the books of Esther, Ezra and Nehemiah.

One thing is for sure, many men and women in the Bible came to discover and understand that there is a God in Heaven. Many rejected the ways of the one true God. We learn the consequences of rejecting God through the experiences of those who would not submit to God's sovereignty.

In the Bible, many learned to love, serve and obey God. Their successful testimonies have become our examples for living throughout history, even today. As our Bible heroes began to know and follow God in the fullness of truth, so can we. For those who receive God as Father, Christ as Lord, and Holy Spirit as Helper, God expresses agape love and divine sovereignty.

In God's many expressions, titles and names, God's character is revealed. To name a few we can come to know God as "Adonai" [The Boss], "Christ" [The Redeemer], "Paraclete" [The Holy Spirit, Teacher and Comforter], "The Way, The Truth and The Life," [Jesus], and "Abba" [God, our heavenly Father in Christ].

For those who receive God as Abba, in the fullness of God's loving grace and commandments through the shed blood of Jesus the Christ—they become not only God's creations, but we also become "children of God."

Also, we must ever be mindful that God is not a "he." God is not a man. God is a Spirit. In the Christian faith, for those of us who receive God as Abba, God is known as "He." In His earthly life, Jesus Christ was God in the body of a human male. Holy Spirit is also often referenced as "He." Yet, please don't be turned away from God by the human efforts to define God.

"God is not a man, so he does not lie. He is not human, so he does not change his mind. Has he ever spoken and failed to act? Has he ever promised and not carried it through?"
(Numbers 23:19 NLT)

"God [is] a spirit; and they who worship him must worship [him] in spirit and truth." (John 4:24 DBT)

The Hidden Prophets Must Speak Out!

Here, in the 21st century, the kingly and priestly anointing arise together. With the Esthers, Daniels, Nehemiahs, and Ezras—we meet the prophetic. We see Obadiah's hidden prophets emerging from the caves to join Elijah as Jezebel and Ahab are defeated.

During America's 2016 elections, we experienced a season where Jezebel had fallen. "They killed us but they ain't whipped us yet…" according to the report by one candidate, Tim Kaine.

Consequently, we continue advancing God's Kingdom with "thus saying" presenting ourselves to Ahab (and all world government authorities including those in the high places of Ephesians 6:12) so that the latter rain can fall increasingly on the earth (avoiding distractions, yielding always to Father God, championed by Lord Jesus, guided by His Excellency, Holy Spirit):

"It happened many days later that the word of Yahweh came to Elijah in the third year, saying, 'Go, present yourself to Ahab so that I may give rain on the surface of the earth.'"
(1 Kings 18:1 WEB)

It's the season for the "hidden prophets" to speak out:

In the Bible account, Ahab called for Obadiah, his household supervisor. This man, who feared the LORD very much, had taken 100 prophets and had hidden them by fifties in a cave, providing them with food and water when Jezebel was trying to destroy the LORD's prophets.

Let the kings and priests of God arise. Let the prophets and intercessors unite with the high praises of God in our mouths.

In the final analysis, hope springs eternal. Even as the year 2016 was a season for God repairing breaches and unleashing many spiritual gifts to advance His Heavenly Kingdom, I pray that 2017 and beyond will be remembered as the beginning of a new and fresh wave of repentance, healing and forgiveness among families, communities and nations. As hope springs eternal, faith will increase and agape love will grow stronger. As this happens, the repairing, rebuilding, restoring process is all part of God's eternal plan to draw America ever closer to His heart.

May this book be a landmark in the history of 21st Century America, chronicling the REPAIRING THE GATES, REBUILDING THE WALL, RESTORING THE DREAM, and RETURNING TO GOD.

Chapter 1

Making a Difference
in this World

CHAPTER ONE

MAKING A DIFFERENCE IN THIS WORLD

When my little granddaughter was five years old, she sang a new song: "I want to be important, and make a difference in this world." So many people have that same desire. I remember seeing a 53-year-old professional gymnast and contortionist appearing on a television talent show and saying, "I don't know why, but I just want to be famous."

So many people sing, speak, write and dream of being important, famous, noticed, remembered, and maybe even like my granddaughter, they want to make a mark and make a difference in the world. Many people don't even know why they have these desires. In a song, "Keep Climbing," Dr. Wintley Phipps sings that, "God placed a dream within our hearts." My Uncle Martin Luther King, Jr. often spoke the words, "I have a dream."

America once had a dream; it was known as "The American Dream." Even in the midst of all of her problems of sin, racism, poverty, broken hearts and broken families, America once dreamed of a better tomorrow. For many years, God had a wall of protection around America, where the dream grew in the hearts of every generation.

Within God's wall of protection around America, the people shared a common theme: "In God We Trust." During seasons of famine and plenty, war and peace, America remained united by her mantra: "In God We Trust."

Having been born in America in 1951, I can remember the days before prayer was removed from the public square in 1963, and when abortion became legal in 1973. Oh, there were woes and wrongs aplenty, yet America still called on the name of the Lord in those days. But the American Dream began to become cloudy as the wall of protection of "The God in Whom we trusted" began to show cracks in the 1960s.

These changes were mostly reflected in subtle shifts of America's focus on faith and family, to self and materialism. As a result, over the next several decades, we found ourselves facing not only enemies from within but terrors from without our nation. Many may not have recognized it, but the enemy has breached the gate. Our walls have crumbled.

Here in 21st century America, we have thus far found ourselves blaming everyone *but* ourselves for our problems. A spirit of entitlement has been sweeping our nation, causing many to feel and believe that only what one wants matters.

During the 2016 U.S. presidential election, a poll was taken which revealed that over 70% of Christians in America believe that feelings and emotions, not biblical truth, should set the standard for victorious living.[1] In other words, how we *feel* about people or situations should set the tone and determine how we should respond to challenges in life. Isn't that amazing? People want to eliminate reason and truth and replace them with feelings.

Yet, everything is not hopeless. As we learn to escape the traps, boxes, labels and ungodly boundaries of fearful sinful living, we can return to God and experience victory—even in the darkest hours and end-time challenges.

Galatians 4:16, "Am I therefore become your enemy, because I tell you the truth?"

In preparing this chapter, I was constantly plagued with the burden that accompanies the mantle of bearing the conservative label. I find that I resist being painted into a corner and confined in a box that is currently labeled as "conservative." The labels of Conservative and Liberal are just as dangerous and misleading as any other labels. They are ambiguous and subjective, so they don't convey a clear meaning. Then when they are attributed to or appointed to a person or a group, an instant division occurs. Labels prohibit people who often share common beliefs on certain issues from standing together with others who may believe *some* of what they believe, but not everything they believe.

The following definitions[2] should clearly and easily distinguish the group labeled "liberal" from the group labeled "conservative."

Liberal—favorable to progress or reform, as in political or religious affairs.

Progress—a movement toward a goal or to a further or higher stage.

Conservative—having the power or tendency to conserve; preserve.

Reform—the improvement or amendment of what is wrong, corrupt, unsatisfactory, etc.: social reform; spelling reform, to put an end to (abuses, disorders, etc.).

Conserve—to prevent injury, decay, waste, or loss of.

Preserve—to keep alive or in existence; make lasting: to preserve our liberties as free citizens, to keep safe from harm or injury, protect or spare.

Yet, we find that even the definitions overlap, causing one to wonder if *liberal* means conservative and vice versa.

For instance, some stand for protecting the lives of our children at *all* stages of life, beginning with the conception of the 46 chromosomes, and ending at natural death. Pro-lifers are neither preventing nor denying life, liberty and justice; pro-lifers are not holding back liberty of life. So, pro-life can be both liberal and conservative. Oh, what fun it is to play the label game.

My friend Elizabeth explains it this way: "We have driven a lot of cars in our day, some new, some used, and some just mere relics of what once was. At one point when our money was low, we purchased a vehicle that came with those wonderful outdated political bumper stickers. There is nothing like running around with a Carter bumper sticker when George Bush Sr. is in office. So, being naïve as to the tenacity with which these labels are designed to adhere to the surface they are placed on, I figured I could apply some elbow grease and chemicals to get the label off. The next morning after breakfast I went forth, armed with my rubber gloves, scrunchie sponge, soapy water and pure ammonia.

"First, I applied the soapy water liberally and then tried to scrub through the label with a scrunchie sponge—no give. Then I applied pure ammonia, and the only thing that loosed up was the congestion in my head. Next, I went into the kitchen for a razor blade, figuring I could gently get the edges to come loose and then ease the rest of the label off. After about 20 minutes of trying this, the only thing that gave were my rubber gloves, which now had so many bits missing, I had to go get another pair.

"While I was inside I grabbed an extension cord and a hair dryer, assuming that if I heated the sticker, it might come loose. But it never did budge completely; I was able to get bits and pieces of it off, but never the whole thing. It now looked worse than when I started, so since we had only paid $150 for the car, and it already had the seats duct-taped, I dried the chrome bumper off and neatly covered the offending bumper sticker with a piece of gray duct tape, calling the morning a 'wash.'

"As I sat on the porch sipping my iced tea and rocking back and forth in my chair, a light suddenly came on in my mind. I realized that the morning had not been a futile effort at all. There were scores of lessons to be learned from that old bumper sticker.

"First, labels stick. When we, as Christians, label one another, be it our children, our spouse or our fellow man, those labels have a tendency to stick. The more we use them, the greater the intensity of the bond between man and label becomes. We get tired and frustrated that our toddlers have not yet learned to see what is so obvious to us, and suddenly we call them 'stupid,' or 'dumb,' or some other barb that sticks in their minds and begins to grow. We feel insecure or frightened, so we give groups and organizations brands that portray them as the enemy and then wonder why we cannot work together or live together in harmony. We view religions, creeds, ethnic groups and even socio-economic groups as either acceptable or not by criteria that are often based on fear, insecurity, lies and sin. Then, after we have wrongfully judged the groups in question, we resort to labeling them with hateful, demeaning, divisive names that stick. Later, when we find a common cause, we struggle to unite, yet often fail because of distrust, deep wounds, and divisions these labels have bred within us. Labels stick.

"Secondly, labels are hard to remove. Sadly, we often realize our mistake after the toddler has become a young adult.

He's grown up hearing us berate him in anger with labels that each year ingrained a false understanding of himself into the fiber of his heart and character until finally, when we wake up and see what we have done, the damage is so deeply rooted; it will not easily be removed. The economy is a problem, yet another war needs to be addressed; poverty is rampant and spreading, and as a society we need to come together to solve these problems, but the labels are stuck. We don't trust each other. We don't see each other in the light of what we can become but rather in the archaic and hateful labels we have grown up to embrace. So then, our collaborations are weak when we need them to be strong, and we find the ability to stand together for a good cause difficult to nearly impossible when it should be so easy. We want to trust each other, but the labels are sticking. We want to not be afraid, but the labels are sticking. We want to forgive each other, but the labels have bonded deep into our hearts. We want to unite, but the divisions are so many and the labels just will not give. Labels are hard to remove.

"Thirdly, sometimes we just have to put a patch on it and try to move forward in hopes that time will heal. The patch is not pretty. The beauty of the sparkling polished chrome bumper will be forever marred by the patch, but gradually, over time, things change. The bumper gets old and starts peeling and rusting and suddenly a duct tape patch doesn't stand out so much. But it takes a lot of time and sadly, while we can move forward, there will always be damage to some degree, left behind.

"Labels prevent us from loving one another as God has commanded us to do. Labels inhibit us from doing unto others as we would have them do unto us. Labels hinder us from allowing the fruits of the Spirit to flow from our hearts to those around us. Labels ostracize people who are created in God's image and cause us to do what God says is foolish—judging ourselves by others rather than by the law of God. Labels impede the movements of unity, peace and harmony for which our families, our communities, our nation and our world are pleading.

"Labels are something Christians must avoid at all cost. After all, the bumper stickers we are applying in our daily lives adhere to human hearts, not mere cars or buildings. The bond and the subsequent damage runs deep and affects not only individuals but families, communities and nations for generation after generation. The use of labels in our lives must stop—immediately. I hope you remember this thought every time you see a bumper sticker."

After reading and re-reading Elizabeth's analogy, I realized why it took so long for me to write about labels and boxes. I was waiting for her to journal this truth. Labels are divisive, and boxes are restrictive, which is why I resist the label of "conservative."

The practice of accepting and assigning labels and boxes is just as bad as assigning separatism to the human race. This practice is deceptive and dangerous. We are one human race, not separate races and classes divided by skin color. There is no red or black, or white or brown, or yellow race. There is one human race with ethnic distinctions. So when we put people in a "color box," we begin to discriminate, which is sin!

Another practice of labeling and boxing is "restricting God-given gifts" that emerge in people we have stereotyped, labeled and boxed in. For example, can an accountant not also be a poet? Can a scientist not also be a great cook? When we label people according to our understanding of their gifts and talents, we leave no room for God's creativity to abundantly burst forth in multiple streams. I have a friend who is a real estate and investment genius. Yet, he is also a wonderful composer and producer of music. People tend to try to tell him that his music is a nice hobby, but that he should stick to one thing. How sad!

In the beloved community, so named by my uncle, Dr. Martin Luther King, Jr., labels, boxes and separate races don't exist. To continue with the initial theme of this section, the conservative label is not a badge of honor. It is a state of being— a cry for liberty in a world that is hungry for truth. As we continue on through this journey to return to God, let us pray that we move on from labels and boxes into a higher place where love abounds. In this higher place, we can glean patterns for success from the foundations in the Bible.

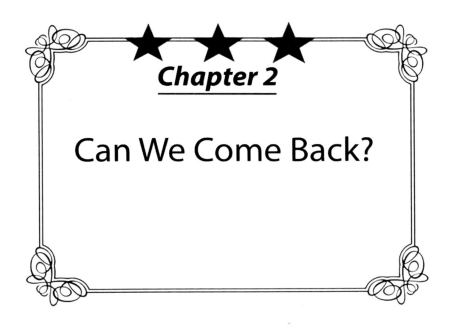

Chapter 2

Can We Come Back?

CHAPTER TWO

CAN WE COME BACK?

At the end of the 20th century, people were preparing for the end of the world as we know it. As the century turned, and the world didn't go up in smoke, America began to have a false sense of security. Then, on September 11, 2001, a terrorist attack breached America's defenses, thus bringing down the World Trade Center's twin towers in New York City. Those buildings represented the symbol of America's wealth and power. The World Trade Center's twin towers were monuments to human accomplishments, often compared by many to the Bible's once famous Tower of Babel.

In the aftermath of the tragedy of the attacks, rather than calling on God, America's leaders played on the feelings and emotions of the people, with promises of rebuilding a greater nation by the might of men. As a result, rather than experiencing a great revival and return to God, America sank more deeply into a morass of tolerance of human error without repentance of sin.

During the months after 9/11, the underground prayerful "Army of God" was not dead; yet the light of the glorious Gospel of Jesus was under attack as never before in America. Thankfully the voices of the prophets of God would not be silenced.

Along these lines, let's examine Rabbi Jonathan Cahn's "The Harbinger" prophecy more closely. Much has been said about his teachings, on the subject. First, here's a recap of the 9/11 era followed by a connection to biblical dots:

"The September 11 attacks (also referred to as 9/11) were a series of four coordinated terrorist attacks by the Islamic terrorist group al-Qaeda on the United States on the morning of September 11, 2001. The attacks killed 2,996 people and injured 6,000 others and caused at least $10 billion in property and infrastructure damage and $3 trillion in total costs..."[1]

It's an understatement to say that America and the world were stunned.

In the aftermath of the fall of the World Trade Center twin towers, both edifices built by human energy as a tribute to amassed wealth, rather than repent for the sins of America, the pride of man rushed to rebuild, starting with "Ground Zero". The demolished World Trade Center site became the new ground zero.[2]

While some considered the original World Trade Center a "modern Tower of Babel," there is much appreciation for the Ground Zero site. Many innocent lives were lost during 9/11 and many agree that it is surely fitting to remember that time as a great loss and tragedy.

While many agree that tribute should be made to the tragedy, there are those who believe that the actions of the United States president during the Ground Zero construction were a connection to Isaiah 9 in the Bible.

In New York City on Thursday, June 14, 2012, President Obama had the chance to personally inscribe a beam that was placed on the top of One Freedom Tower. The skyscraper was designed to replace the fallen Twin Towers in lower Manhattan. In his own handwriting, the president wrote this on the beam: "We remember. We rebuild. We come back stronger!" —Barack Obama. New York Gov. Andrew Cuomo, New Jersey Gov. Chris Christie, and First Lady Michelle Obama also signed the beam.

Many who have read "The Harbinger" or have seen the video documentary "The Isaiah 9:10 Judgment" connect the president's message to Bible prophecy:

"We remember," President Obama wrote. "We rebuild. We come back stronger!"

The book and the video have shocked readers and viewers around the country and the world by showing the eerie and striking parallels between the vows of the leaders of ancient Israel before its judgment and fall and those of American leaders since Sept. 11, 2001. "What was foreshadowed in "The Harbinger" and "The Isaiah 9:10 Judgment" film is now being fulfilled by the President of the United States," says Jonathan Cahn, the messianic rabbi-pastor and author.

The book and film specifically connect President Obama's words from his first State of the Union message in January 2009 with the ancient vow that brought judgment to ancient Israel.

The ancient vow begins with these words: "The bricks have fallen, but we will rebuild with hewn stone,'" explains Cahn. "The vow declares Israel's defiance of God, in the face of a devastating strike on the land. The hewn stone, which begins the rebuilding, symbolizes the nation's intention to come back stronger than before. The book then reveals the parallel a proclamation given by Obama: "I want every American to know this: We will rebuild. And the United States of America will emerge stronger than before," he said.

Rabbi Cahn ties the 9/11 attacks to a section of Isaiah 9, which describes God vowing to destroy ancient Israel for persistent disobedience toward Him and ignoring the warnings He has sent them. One such warning was a military attack on

Israel which caused physical damage to the land. Verses 9 and 10 illustrate that rather than recognize God's warning and repent of its sins, Israel defiantly vowed to rebuild using stronger materials and to plant stronger trees.

"The Lord sent a word into Jacob, and it hath lighted upon Israel. And all the people shall know, even Ephraim and the inhabitant of Samaria, that say in the pride and stoutness of heart, the bricks are fallen down, but we will build with hewn stones: the sycamores are cut down, but we will change them into cedars. Therefore, the Lord shall set up the adversaries of Rezin against him, and join his enemies together; The Syrians before, and the Philistines behind; and they shall devour Israel with open mouth. For all this his anger is not turned away, but his hand is stretched out still." (Isaiah 9:8-12 KJV)

Note: when called to repent by God, the Israelites defied God and went on in their own strength (Isaiah 9:10). They refused to repent. A remarkable parallel occurs surrounding 9/11. Even though the prophets of America were calling for prayer and repentance after the attacks, the political leaders of America were bent on vowing to rebuild by the strength of manpower. There was no national cry for repentance from America's political corridors.

President Obama signed the beam on June 14, when he and the First Lady toured the One World Trade Center site. According to the *Associated Press*, the beam was sealed into the structure of the building and was not visible when the construction of the tower was completed.

The prevailing attitudes of America's leaders after 9/11 and the subsequent rebuilding reflect these passages in Isaiah 9:8-17 (MSG):

"The Master sent a message against Jacob. It landed right on Israel's doorstep. All the people soon heard the message, Ephraim and the citizens of Samaria. But they were a proud and arrogant bunch. They dismissed the message, saying, 'Things aren't that bad. We can handle anything that comes. If our buildings are knocked down, we'll rebuild them bigger and finer. If our forests are cut down, we'll replant them with finer trees.'"

"So GOD incited their adversaries against them, stirred up their enemies to attack: From the east, Arameans; from the west, Philistines. They made hash of Israel. But even after that, He was still angry, His fist still raised, ready to hit them again."

"But the people paid no mind to Him who hit them, didn't seek GOD -of-the-Angel-Armies. So GOD hacked off Israel's head and tail, palm branch and reed, both on the same day. The big-head elders were the head; the lying prophets were the tail. Those who were supposed to lead this people led them down blind alleys, and those who followed the leaders ended up lost and confused. That's why the Master lost interest in the young men, had no feeling for their orphans and widows. All of them were godless and evil, talking filth and folly. And even after that, he was still angry, his fist still raised, ready to hit them again."

Thankfully, God's praying Church was underground during this season; with prayer movements abounding across the nation (nations. By the grace of God, the prayers reached Heaven and the hearts of leaders and citizens alike began to awaken and turn back to God. Inspired by God's Holy Spirit, "If movements" began to spring up across America.

"If my people, who are called by my name, will humble themselves and pray and seek my face and turn from their wicked ways, then I will hear from heaven, and I will forgive their sin and will heal their land." (2 Chronicles 7:14 NIV)

Because God is ever faithful and ever merciful, He caused the voices of His prophets to become amplified with proclamations such as "the Church can turn the tide." Twentieth century prayer ministries moved to the forefront in America. New prayer movements began to spring up everywhere. As a counter voice to the secular "Rebuild movement," the spiritual "Repent movement" surged.

There is an urgent cry in the spirit today, to the lost and wandering soul that is desperate to be rescued and brought into God's light. The pressing question, "Can we come back to God?" remains, and is amplified by another, "How?"

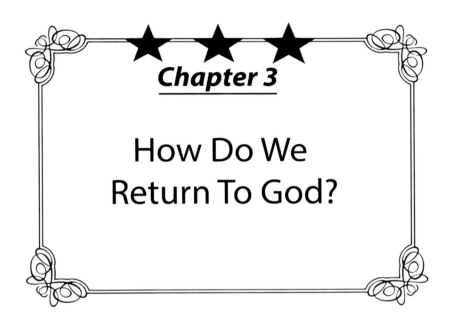

Chapter 3

How Do We Return To God?

CHAPTER THREE

HOW DO WE RETURN TO GOD?

I recently spoke at a conference where social justice and social ills were being discussed. Our panel of community organizers presented various models for rebuilding the communities of America. Each of our models included programs that were faith-based, with God being an interactive part of the intervention and rebuilding process.

At the end of the panel discussion, the floor was opened up for questions and answers. The last question became a diatribe with the speaker spewing anger and frustration peppered with profanity. Her last words were that "you people come here every year with how you help your little organizations help a handful of people, while whole communities are dying. Each of you needs to pack your bags and go to Washington, DC and demand that our government protects us and rescues our nation from all of the disasters we are facing."

As the distressed and disenchanted woman droned on about her woes and America's ills, it became apparent that she hadn't really understood much of the testimony of the panelists during the earlier presentation. Each of us had given several examples of how, by the grace and intervention of God, we had been used to rescue homeless people, convicted offenders, young people and many others from difficult circumstances. We panelists made it very clear that God would be the driving force behind restoring our communities. Yet, it remained very apparent that this woman felt like governments and humans are the saviors of the world. There was a major disconnect. She didn't realize that God was *needed* in bringing to pass deliverance for our communities.

Not only did she reflect the perspective that a large populous of humanity has turned away from God, she was reflecting that there is a world who maybe doesn't know God at all. It may sound amazing, but there is an entire generation that doesn't even realize that they have left God.

The book of Malachi best defines the problem:

"From the days of your fathers you have turned aside from my statutes and have not kept them. Return to me, and I will return to you, says the Lord of hosts. But you say, 'How shall we return?'" (Malachi 3:7 ESV).

Therein is the problem. Many people are not aware that they have even left the Lord.

In 2002, Pastor Stephen Muncherian wrote: "In order to understand the question (of how we can return to God), it's important for us to see that (in Malachi) God's people didn't realize that they had left God. According to them they were doing all the right things—they believed in God, they were going up to the temple and to all the services; offering sacrifices and making donations. So, when God said, 'Return,' they said, 'How? How can we return if we've never left?'

"So many Christians today are asking the same question because they don't realize that they've left God. The call to return is met with disbelief, skepticism and sometimes even anger. (Many) People (are) doing religiously what they know how to do.

"All of these things are not wrong. They have their place and their value. But, we can do all these things and still miss the heart of God's call to His people to live in a personal, blessed relationship with Him."[1]

Dr. J. Vernon McGee in his commentary on Malachi writes this, "Ritualism has been substituted for reality. Pageantry has been substituted for power. The aesthetic has been substituted for the spiritual, and form for feeling. Even in the orthodox, conservative, and evangelical circle, they know the vocabulary, but the power of God is gone."[2]

This is a danger we face today—having a form of godliness, yet denying the power of God. Too many do not realize that we have moved away from God. So before we can go any further in returning to God, we must admit that we have left God.

Next, we must do as instructed in 2 Chronicles 7:14: "If my people, which are called by my name, shall humble themselves, and pray, and seek my face, and turn from their wicked ways; then will I hear from heaven, and will forgive their sin, and will heal their land" (KJV).

Yes, this is the formula for returning to God:

1. Realize that we have turned away from God.
2. Humble ourselves.
3. Pray.
4. Seek God's face.
5. Turn away from our wicked ways by repenting of our sins and our abandonment of God.

For further study, we can look to the books of Ezra, Nehemiah and Esther. In these three books, we have the templates to come out of captivity, back to God.

Once we are back in the will of God, in humble obedience to God's directions and instructions, we are ready to move forward.

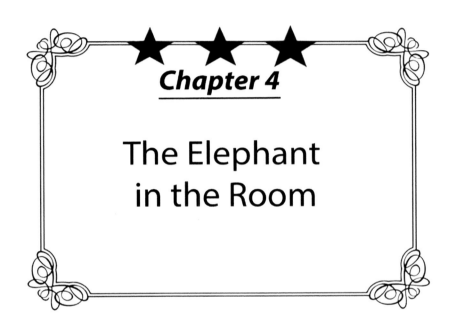

Chapter 4

The Elephant in the Room

CHAPTER FOUR

THE ELEPHANT IN THE ROOM

I'm not sure how much further we can go along the road to repenting, rebuilding, repairing, restoring and returning to God here in America, until we face the giant elephant in the room—racism and subsequent white privilege. Pastor Mike Berry introduced this monster in his foreword. I really appreciate Pastor Mike's boldness. As a Caucasian preacher in 21st century America, he could very well have chosen to sit back, utter platitudes, and look the other way like so many of his peers still do.

During our conversations about "white privilege," I often marvel that Pastor Mike is among the now growing number of Americans who "get it." It is not about reparation checks for black people. It is not about fanning the flames of victimization to a fever pitch until blood runs down our streets. It is about repenting and correcting the flawed and corrupt system that has ruled America for far too long.

What is Racial Colorblindness?

Racial issues are often uncomfortable to discuss and rife with stress and controversy. Many ideas have been advanced to address this sore spot in the American psyche. Currently, the most pervasive approach is known as colorblindness. Colorblindness is the racial ideology that posits the best way to end discrimination is by treating individuals as equally as possible, without regard to race, culture, or ethnicity.

At its face value, colorblindness seems like a good thing—really taking MLK Jr. seriously on his call to judge people on the content of their character rather than the color of their skin. It focuses on commonalities between people, such as their shared humanity.

However, according to Monnica T. Williams, Ph.D., "Colorblindness alone is not sufficient to heal racial wounds on a national or personal level. It is only a half-measure that in the end operates as a form of racism."

For the record, before we go any further, no human being is literally black or white. Even the palest ivory Caucasian skin has beige or pearl undertones. Even the most ebony hue has undertones of purple, blue and magenta. There are varying skin colors in human beings as in almost everything in creation and under the sun. So where does this "color blind" concept really find its deceptive source?

"I Once Was Blind, But Now I See!" (see John 9:25)

In the biological sense, if someone is "color blind" they are considered to have a design flaw. There are various medical treatments for such a condition. Yet, here in 21st century America, when discussing issues of race, there is a popular politically correct phrase: "I don't see color. I am color blind." On the surface, this sounds so sweet and kind, doesn't it? Well, in a spiritual sense, such a condition is vitriol, and those with the condition need spiritual enlightenment.

Why? Because RACIAL COLOR BLINDNESS IS SPIRITUAL BLINDNESS, which gives cover to the system that fosters white privilege.

How Is White Privilege Defined?

According to Tim Wise, Antiracist Essayist: "White privilege refers to any advantage, opportunity, benefit, head start, or general protection from negative societal mistreatment, which persons deemed white will typically enjoy, but which others will generally not enjoy. These benefits can be material (such as greater opportunity in the labor market, or greater net worth, due to a history in which whites had the ability to accumulate wealth to a greater extent than persons of color), social (such as presumptions of competence, creditworthiness, law-abidingness, intelligence, etc.) or psychological (such as not having to worry about triggering negative stereotypes, rarely having to feel out of place, not having to worry about racial profiling, etc.) ...

"...And these other forms of privilege exist—and generally provide greater opportunity to their respective group members—even though there are rich people who lead miserable lives despite their money, and there are men, heterosexuals, Christians, and able-bodied folks who are poor. On balance, it pays to be a member of any of those dominant groups. And the same is true with (so called) whiteness."[1]

One Race, Human: Many Ethnicities

"Of one blood, God made all human beings to live on the face of the earth." (see Acts 17:26)

The human race is often manifested by various skin colors, body types, hair types and other cultural and ethnic distinctions. God *never* intended for these God-approved distinctions to divide human communities.

It's Not About Skin Tone–It's About Our Blood

On August 28, 2010, I stood on the steps of the Lincoln Memorial in Washington, DC before an audience of an estimated half a million listeners and said that "I too have a dream." Six years later, in the sweltering, hot summer of 2016, "Black Lives Matter" became the predominant inflammatory moniker until the phrase "white privilege" became the power chant of choice, causing a relatively ancient enemy to create a new uproar. Both black lives matter and accusations of white privilege are highly inflammatory chants, no doubt; but is it really at the core of the dissension?

Simply put, it's the notion that white people are entitled to certain things—like the benefit of the doubt—merely because of their skin, while in many cases, Black Americans are not.

In 2016, America reached a boiling point, becoming more deeply divided over the relentless killings of unarmed black men by police officers, and the retaliatory random killings of police officers across the nation. In the onslaught, as a minister of the Gospel of Jesus Christ, the niece of Martin Luther King Jr., and a pro-life activist, I am often called on to address a connection between white privilege and the mantra that blacks in America don't matter.

From my point of view, the sanctity of life is nested in the core of the conflict. Understanding this, I also feel obliged to continually note that abortion simmers in the fray, and it is abortion healing that will be a key to overcoming the evil system of white privilege.

While the skin color issues, which first manifested in the 18th and 19th century, American enslavement of blacks from Africa split the nation, the continued struggle for total abolition of slavery in America continues to have the same divisive effect. Since the founding of America, there has been a generational caste/skin color system in the nation, which was instilled in its inception to manage the population growth of the various "working classes" who were drafted as slaves and indentured servants to build and sustain the labor of the country.

Even though from 2008 to 2016 a black man presided in the U. S. Oval Office, racism is still with us in America. Unbelievably, from the inception of his administration, America's "first black president" signed on to expand federal tax-supported funding for abortion, which is noted as "the war on the wombs of women and their offspring." Consequently, America's 44th President leaves a legacy which includes being the greatest presidential abortion champion that America has ever known. If he and America's 21st century female nominee for the U. S. presidency, along with other political leaders in high places have their way, abortion will be an American staple for countless generations to come. Following the lead of their hero, racist Planned Parenthood founder Margaret Sanger, America's black president and radical women's lib supporters, are trying to abolish the civil rights of Americans from the womb to the tomb.

Racism explains why the eugenicist Margaret Sanger began the Negro Project to push contraceptives and prevent blacks from bearing children. Racism explains why the organization she spawned, Planned Parenthood, sets up shop more often than not in minority neighborhoods, selling abortion as a solution to poverty and all the problems that come with it — unemployment, crime, incarceration, just to name a few. And racism explains why a disproportionate number of children who never make it out of the womb alive are black. Racism and abortion are two parts of the three-headed monster that are out to devour the United States as we know it (the third is sexual perversion, a topic for another day).

The following testimonies reveal that African-Americans are not the only victims of racism in the U.S.

A pro-life activist recalls growing up as a Cuban American in the 1980s: "Neighbors called us dirty Mexicans. There were once some robberies nearby and police asked neighborhood boys about my brothers. One neighbor set their dog loose on my sister who had biked by their house. She barely got away. This was an affluent white suburban neighborhood. Consequently, as children, we learned to 'pass for white' to avoid and avert violence and harm."

Another pro-life soldier has a beautiful testimony about blood: "My parents wanted to abort me. I survived the attempt. As a newborn, I required life-saving blood transfusions. Two men—an African-American and an Arab—willingly donated the blood that saved this white baby's life. They were human donors, not different races from me. To save my life, the only color that mattered was that red blood. Later in my life, another kind of blood transfusion saved me forever. On a night consumed with thoughts of suicide, Jesus lifted me up and welcomed me into His one-blood family."

Yet another explains white privilege this way: "As a pro-life advocate, I witness firsthand the imbalance of abortions in the black community. It's not because blacks are more immoral than other ethnic communities. We see the same type of imbalance in the justice system. My brother and I grew up in a neighborhood where many African-American males were incarcerated as teenagers for offenses that guys of other ethnic groups received a slap on the wrist for. My brother says the higher incarceration rates for blacks are because sentencing is often stronger when they get to court, and socioeconomic factors prevent them from being able to afford good legal representation. He is convinced this is by design rather than happenstance."

As we can see from the testimonies here, there is an awakening regarding the "one blood"—that we are not separate races breaking out across America and around the world. Many people consider these occurrences across the ages to be serendipitous, accidental, and unrelated. Yet, where peripherals collide, convergence is imminent. God is the Master Orchestrator. He moves on the hearts of His people to pray and repent. Then God heals us.

We can argue about whose lives matter more or who enjoys more privileges, but that won't end racism. It's only when we recognize the bond that Jesus' blood forges for us that we will end racial hatred—and the violence that tears an innocent child from his mother's womb—and learn to see that we are more united in our humanity than we are divided by the color of our skin.

One Blood, One Race—
See Humanity Through God's Eyes!

Color blindness (also called race blindness) is a sociological term for the disregard of racial characteristics when selecting which individuals will participate in some activity or receive some service. It is politically correct but spiritually incorrect because we are one blood (see Acts 17:26).

When evolutionary biologists, geneticists, and zoologists apply the same criteria to humans that they use to sub-classify all other forms of animal life on this planet, the overwhelming majority of them conclude that the concept of race/subspecies completely fails as a description of human diversity. The biological concept of race has been rejected by the scientific majority. Unfortunately, the sociological concept of race lives on, founded on false concepts of biological race. The Bible has always rejected the concept of race in its entirety. Acts 17 asserts that the idea of biological race is pure fiction. Jesus's teachings on the Golden Rule prove that the concept of sociological race is a grievous sin. Sin ultimately produces death, so it is no surprise that people have always died and will continue to die as long as the myth of race lives on.

Ending Racism in America

*"Of one blood, God created all people [in His image]
to dwell on the face of the earth." (see Acts 17:26)*

"We must learn to live together as brothers [and sisters] or perish as fools." —Dr. Martin Luther King, Jr.

Flawed attempts to cure racial, class and caste disparities in America continue to divide us. It is time to wake up and unite as the human race, something my uncle, Martin Luther King, Jr., called *The Beloved Community*.

America was founded using several classes of labor. Among these labor pools were forced enslavement of Native Africans, attempted enslavement of Native Americans, indentured servants, sharecroppers, and other forms of labor pools. Some of these "classes" evolved from the feudal systems of the world; some from the practice of enslaving people outside of clans and tribes. Throughout its history, America has attempted to cure these practices with various laws and initiatives. Below see seven categories delineating flawed efforts to cure the age-old issues of racism in America:

Abolishing Slavery—Past and Present (Negro slaves, babies in the womb): Abolitionism is a movement to end slavery, whether formal or informal. In Western Europe and the Americas, abolitionism is a historical movement to end the African and Indian slave trade and set slaves free.

Emancipation Proclamation

The Emancipation Proclamation was a presidential proclamation and executive order issued by President Abraham Lincoln on January 1, 1863. In a single stroke, it changed the federal legal status of more than 3 million enslaved people in the designated areas of the South from "slave" to "free". It had the practical effect that as soon as a slave escaped the control of the Confederate government, by running away or through advances of federal troops, the slave became legally free. Eventually, it reached and liberated all of the designated slaves. It was issued as a war measure during the American Civil War, directed to all of the areas in rebellion and all segments of the executive branch of the United States.

American Indian Reservations

In 1876, President Ulysses S. Grant strengthened Indian Reservations in order to help settle the growing conflict between the Native Americans and the early settlers. There has always been a great deal of conflict and controversy about Indian reservations and how they came about. The truth is that the Native Americans were here first and Indian reservations were set up to give them a piece of land, while the settlers set up new rules and laws and took over the land. Some of the new laws had prohibited the Native Americans from hunting and continuing life in the manner they were accustomed to. Besides hunting, many of the early settlers were setting up new plans to convert the Native Americans to Christianity. However, without the ability to hunt and gather food, as they were accustomed to, many of the Native Americans became bitter as they were forced off their lands and told to become farmers. Many of the early Indian reservations were resistant to farming and some of the Native Americans faced starvation.

Reconstruction Era

The term *Reconstruction Era*, in the context of the history of the United States, has two senses: the first covers the complete history of the entire country from 1865 to 1877 following the Civil War; the second sense focuses on the transformation of the Southern United States from 1863 to 1877, as directed by Congress, with the reconstruction of state and society.

Women's Rights

Past Suffragette Movement; and present women's reproductive issues.

White Privilege

White Privilege (or white skin privilege) is a term for societal privileges that benefit people identified as white in Western countries, beyond what is commonly experienced by non-white people under the same social, political, or economic circumstances (often dictated, managed and controlled by social security prefixes, zip code designations, etc.).

Redlining

In the United States, redlining is the practice of denying services, either directly or through selectively raising prices, to residents of certain areas based on the racial or ethnic makeups of those areas.

It doesn't end there—there are debates over:

- Artificial Birth Control.
- Abortion Rights.
- Black Privilege—Special rights to blacks assigned because of skin color.
- Affirmative Action—Special rights to black and other minorities assigned because of skin color or ethnicity.

- Minority Set-Asides—Special rights to blacks and other ethnicities assigned because of skin color and ethnicity.
- Gender Rights.
- Black Lives Matter.
- All Lives Matter.

Even the once acceptable justification of racial division among God's family is being debunked. God never divided people according to skin color. When God instructs His people in the Bible not to marry aliens or foreigners, this is not a skin color racial issue; it is a spiritual matter, as in, "Believers don't marry and procreate with devil and demon worshipers [becoming unequally yoked]."

Classic Bible Examples: Ruth and Naomi were from different nations and ethnic groups (not races). Ruth accepted Naomi's God (our God), and was blessed to become a member of King David's and the Lord Jesus' family. The Gentile woman who told Jesus the Jew, "Even the dogs eat the crumbs..." was a human being, one race. In these and many other instances, there have been ethnic distinctions among the nations resulting in people erroneously considered others to be of different "races."

Modern History: "I have a dream that my four little children will one day live in a nation where they will not be judged by the color of their skin but by the content of their character." Rev. Martin Luther King, Jr.

In 1958, Dr. Billy Graham and my uncle, Dr. Martin Luther King, Jr., appeared together and prayed at a revival meeting in New York City. They agreed that the most sacred hour in America at the time was eleven o'clock on Sunday mornings, where for the most part, American Christians gathered in their racially divided communities to attend church services. Of course, there were exceptions to this rule, but there always are. Dr. Graham and Dr. King made a bold move to step outside of the walls of the traditional church into the mainstream of America.

Interestingly enough, a deranged Negro woman stabbed Uncle M.L. in the chest with a letter opener during that

(Pictured: Martin Luther King Jr. with Reverend Billy Graham)

visit. She didn't understand or agree with his message of *one race, one beloved community*. She thought he was committing a crime against humanity by considering it acceptable to call Dr. Graham his equal, his brother. The same can be said for many who felt the same way about Dr. Graham.

It was the love of God in the heart of Dr. King during those days that rescued him from the operating table to live to write the 1963 "Letter from a Birmingham Jail," which brought the inequity of the church pews of America to an even larger audience. Again, Uncle MLK was praying and fighting for the walls of injustice to come down and be replaced with the covering and protection of the grace of God for all Americans, and all people. This was the "Beloved Community" of MLK, my father Rev. A. D. King (his brother), and the entire "King Family Legacy," and indeed many Americans and people around the world.

"United Cry: A Reconciled Church!"
by Will Ford

This is an update regarding the powerful repentance portion of "United Cry DC 2016" at the Lincoln Memorial in Washington, DC. April 9th, 2016, which will go down as the day God was focusing on "healing a divided nation and uniting the Church." April 9th, at different times in history, has been significantly used to address division and bring unity.

For example, most are familiar with the fact that April 9th, 1865 was the day the South surrendered to the North in the Civil War. In 1857, many felt a Supreme Court decision sealed the fate of enslaved African Americans. In Dred Scott v. Sandford, Supreme Court justices ruled by a 7-2 decision that slaves were the property of their masters—with no human rights and no representation in court. However, because of prayer and acts of obedience, hearts changed, and eventually this demonic decree was broken over America. Revival was released and justice came in the form of a civil war, which ended April 9th, 1865, ultimately ending slavery in America.

Forty-one years later on another April 9th, the Azusa Street Revival started in 1906. This was a revival that united the races in Christ like never before. Native Americans, Asians, Whites, Hispanics and African Americans all were present at Azusa Street. During a time when America was suffering from division after reconstruction, God used a united Church to heal a divided nation through this powerful outpouring of the Holy Spirit.

Another significant event on April 9th happened in 1968. It was the date of Civil Rights leader Martin Luther King Jr.'s funeral. In his "I Have a Dream" speech, Dr. King said he dreamed of the day when "...the sons of former slaves, and the sons of former slave owners, could sit down together at the table of brotherhood." God is serious in this season of the Church uniting together because He hasn't forgotten about this God-given dream, which is rooted in Jesus' prayer of John 17, that God's "glory would come, and make us one so that the world will believe."

This was providentially made clear to me through the relationship of my dear friend Matt Lockett, Director of Bound 4 Life and The Justice House of Prayer in Washington, DC. We actually met on MLK Celebration Day, January 17th, 2005, where I was speaking at a conference in Washington, DC. Before we had the conference that night, we had a prayer gathering at the Lincoln Memorial, where Dr. King gave his famous speech.

A Past Connection

It was at that prayer meeting that my friend Matt Lockett and I first met each other. We then talked for the first time after I spoke that night at Hope Christian Church. Matt eventually left corporate America, and moved to DC, taking over Bound4Life and Justice House of Prayer in DC, and we became very good friends over the past eleven years. We didn't know, however, that God had more in store for us, through our family heritage.

It takes a book to chronicle the amazing ways the Lord led us on this journey of discovery. I can only highlight a few of the remarkable ways God connected us. First, about two years ago, Matt made the incredible discovery that on April 6th, 1865, the last Civil War battle of General Robert E. Lee (which brought about the surrender of General Lee on April 9, 1865), happened at a farmhouse called Lockett Farm in Virginia.

Matt found out that he is a direct descendant of those same Locketts. In other words, over 150 years ago, the Civil War ended in Matt's family's front yard! Another amazing discovery we made is that Matt's family owned many slaves in Virginia, Louisiana, and other states. After a year of research by both of us, we are certain through empirical evidence, that Matt's family owned my family during the time of slavery. This takes on a deeper meaning when you understand the well-documented story of how the slaves in my family prayed for freedom.

It's for this reason that a 200-year-old black kettle pot has been passed down by my Christian slave forbearers in Lake Providence, Louisiana. While used for cooking and washing clothes during the day, this kettle was secretly used for prayer. Forbidden to pray by their slave master, my ancestors were beaten unmercifully if found doing so. However, in spite of their master's cruelty, and because of their love for Jesus, they prayed anyway. At night, sneaking into a barn, they carried this cast iron cooking pot into their secret prayer meeting. As others looked out, those inside prayed.

Turning this pot upside-down on the barn floor, they propped it up with rocks—suspending the pot a few inches above the ground. Then, while lying prostrate or kneeling on the ground, they prayed in a whisper underneath the kettle to muffle their voices. The story passed down with the kettle is that they were risking their lives to pray for the next generation.

Once freedom came, an unknown teenage girl decided to keep this pot and pass it down along with the story of how others prayed for our freedom. She passed the story and the kettle down to Harriet Lockett; who then passed it on to Nora

Lockett, who then passed it on to William Ford Sr., who gave it to William Ford Jr. — who then gave it to me, William Ford III. I learned that my forefathers were originally slaves in Virginia, but were then sent to a plantation in Lake Providence, Louisiana, the city where my father was born.

Though this kettle was only used as an acoustic means to keep their prayers from being heard, it's been passed down in our family as a reminder of the prayer bowls in Heaven of Revelation 5:8. Amazingly, God heard the whispered prayers of Lockett slaves in Louisiana, and with His shout, ended slavery in the front yard of the family that owned them at Lockett Farm in Virginia.

Nevertheless, being the God of the past and the future, He then connected two sons from those same family lines together, to war against injustice in their day, and cry out in prayer for awakening in their time.

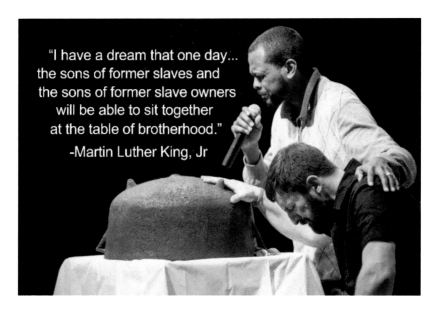

(Pictured: Will Ford with Matt Lockett)

What Storyline Do You Want to Be a Part Of?

Matt and I have been awed, stunned and wept together as Christian brothers over what God has revealed to us. And mind you, we first met each other on MLK Celebration Day, at the Lincoln Memorial, where Dr. King said in his speech that he dreamed of the day when "sons of former slaves and the sons of former slave owners will be able to sit together at the table of brotherhood."

We also learned that God wasn't only answering my forefather's prayers for freedom, but also the prayers of one of Matt's forefathers as well. Matt also discovered that one of his forefathers preached the Gospel with Francis Asbury and was a revivalist and abolitionist against slavery. You see, all of us in America have generational curses and generational blessings we can connect to in our families, in our regions, even in our nation.

The question God has before the nation and the Church is this: Are we going to be a part of the healing or the hurt? The blessing or the curse? God is asking us: "What storyline do you want to be a part of?"

Matt and I met on the day America celebrates the dreamer, Dr. King, because God has a dream He wants to fulfill. It's the prayer He's still answering from His Son from John 17, that the "...glory would come, and make us one, so that the world would believe." With the current racial tension in our nation today, this April 9th, on the anniversary of Dr. King's burial, I believe God was saying that if we don't deal with our division, the dream can't live on.

United Cry DC 2016

In an effort to address this, Matt and I participated in one of the most powerful reconciliation efforts I've been a part of in twenty years of ministry. It was during the national prayer meeting, United Cry DC 2016, which took place on April 9, 2016, at the Lincoln Memorial. Aware of the significance of this date, the organizers, Lewis and Rachel Hogan, connected with Bishop Harry Jackson and historian Mike Berry.

(Photo of Bill Haley, Rev. Lynn Jackson, Rev. Bernice King and Dr. Alveda King at United Cry 2016)

Through much prayer and the leading of the Holy Spirit, they were able to assemble the following people to be part of the repentance portion of this prayer gathering: The great-granddaughter of Dred Scott, Lynn Jackson; Bill Haley, descendant of Kunta Kinte who is also the grandson of Alex Haley, author of Roots. Also present from the King family were Dr. Alveda King, daughter of Rev. A.D. King, and Dr. Bernice King, daughter of Dr. Martin Luther King, Jr.

As we sat in chairs on a stage at the Lincoln Memorial, water was poured into the kettle pot used by my forefathers for prayer, then collected in small pitchers for this solemn foot washing. Symbolically pouring water over our feet, prayers of forgiveness were made. First, to the King family, there was repentance for not comforting them during their season of grieving. Not only were Dr. King and his brother Rev. A. D. King assassinated, but their mother, Mrs. Alberta Williams King, was shot and killed in an assassination plot.

Just as important, prayers of forgiveness and repentance were made to the King family, for the Church not stewarding their father's God-given dream to fight for justice, unity and brotherly love. As intercessors, they received this act of contrition and forgiveness and prayed for the healing of our nation. In the midst of this, other pastors washed the feet of Bill Haley and Lynn Jackson.

As this went on, Matt Lockett and I washed each other's feet, at the spot where we first met. We were moved to tears. Mind you, this was all done at the spot where Dr. King said he dreamed of the day when, "...sons of former slaves and the sons of former slave owners will be able to sit together at the table of brotherhood." You see, God has used April 9th to make us one: In 1865 He used a Civil War; in 1906, He used a revival through Azusa Street; and in 1968, He used a reformer as a seed, Dr. King, to birth a new movement of love and unity that would spring up today.

After this, the Reconciled Church, a coalition led by Bishop Harry Jackson, awarded several national leaders the "Dr. Martin Luther King, Jr. Mantle of Destiny Award" from "The King Family Legacy Foundation." It was given to recognize leaders that have worked for years to heal the race issue in America. We were charged to make disciples that would do justice, heal and reconcile today, as the King family prayed for those being mantled to continue on the work begun by their fathers, but started by Jesus in John 17.

Prophetically, though I was one of the proud recipients, there has been a new mantle released to us all. God hasn't abandoned this dream because He hasn't abandoned His Son's prayer of John 17: "That Your glory may come, and make them one, so that the world will believe."[2]

William Ford III, Director, Marketplace Leadership
Christ for the Nations Institute

Three Witnesses

Along with the letter above from Will Ford, there are three additional testimonies from friends who have experienced this "white privilege" controversy from the corridors of having been born with "white skin." They are identified by their initials rather than their full names.

CC writes: One Blood Transfusion:

In our humanity, we see each other through the color of our skin. I've learned there is much under the skin, that many of us do not realize, making us truly "One Blood."

I've pondered my own story as I've reflected upon recent days in our nation and as I've ministered to women and babies for the past 30 years. What we think separates us can be the one thing that unites us…brings us together as one.

I can remember seeing photos of myself, as a newborn baby, with a needle attached to a tube on the side of my head. The needle was administering either needed blood or medication so that I would live. I remember the look of anguish on my tiny face. I looked helpless.

As a child, I asked my mother, "What happened to me?" She told me, "Some things had happened during the pregnancy and shortly after you were born, a nurse noticed you were very blue. You were rushed to another hospital and they had to do a complete blood transfusion."

I was told in order for me to receive the transfusion that would save my life, two men, one of African and Arabic heritage, had donated their blood. They had willingly given their blood and their blood had saved my life.

There I was, a helpless baby, not knowing that I even needed a blood transfusion. I also didn't care who would donate the blood. I was crying out for my life. In my helplessness and inability to speak, another person stepped in to save my life.

God had given me the desire to live and from the beginning, He was protecting me. He had compelled both the men of African and Arabic heritage to give their blood so I could live. Now, under my white skin, I was carrying their blood in my veins. Their blood saved my life.

As I grew up and years went by, continued words of rejection, sexual abuse, my deep need for love and acceptance, and my subsequent wrong choices, led me to make decisions that repeated a cycle of destruction (abortion, alcohol, drugs, destructive relationships) almost to the point of death. I needed a spiritual rescue, intervention and a blood transfusion of my soul and my spirit.

I remember the day. Actually, it begins with the night before. I thought of taking my life but God kept me awake. I know that now. There must have been another great battle for my life that night.

The following morning, I was invited to a place where people learned to love God...and were transformed by His love...where people looked beneath my skin and saw my broken soul. The people were from all cultures and colors...black, white, yellow, olive, brown...and a few tattooed with purple, gold, black, blue, and green. They accepted me. Many had walked the same walk of life...before they walked the aisle.

That day, they took my hand and led me to the One who unites us all. His Name is Jesus. He rescued me that day and gave me the spiritual and soul blood transfusion that would give me new life and save me from death—forever. Another Man, Jesus of Nazareth—who gave His life, who saw me in my nakedness as a baby, helpless in my broken soul and wrong choices as an adult—took my sin and shame. He came to rescue me, to save me, and give me His unconditional love. He gave His life and His blood so that I would live. His "One Blood" now transfused to each one of us who will believe.

Now, I had come into a family of One Blood. The One Blood family of Jesus, the family of God, of many cultures and colors—black, brown, white, yellow, olive and tattooed. The blood transfusion of Jesus Christ is for everyone who will surrender their life to Him and believe that Jesus is Lord, the King of Kings, Savior, Healer of our broken souls, and the soul of our nation. Receive His forgiveness and new life.

In Christ, we are One Blood. We have His blood through transfusion.

I sense when we get to Heaven, we will be surprised at the heritage we've each carried under our skin. It is time for us, as Christians, to love with the love of Jesus—to look through our skin and see the blood of Jesus through our cultures and colors. We are His beautiful people, His brothers and sisters, and His family.

Jesus' blood heals, forgives, gives life, bonds us together in love as family.

We are One Blood—transfused with the forgiving, transforming love of Jesus.

Humanity turns from God and kingdoms crumble. Humans repent and turn back to God and lives and lands are restored. —end of CC testimony.

It's Not About Skin Tone—It's About Our Blood

In early 21st century America, "Black Lives Matter" became a conflicted chant, while throughout America's history the phrase "white privilege" has remained a thorn in her flesh. All of this is inflammatory language no doubt, but what does it mean? Simply put, it's the misguided notion that in general, white people are entitled to certain things—like the benefit of the doubt—merely because of the color of their skin, regardless of the content of their character.

During the 2016 presidential elections, America became deeply divided over the killing of unarmed black men by police and the retaliatory killing of police officers. As the niece of Martin Luther King Jr., and a pro-life activist, I have often been called upon to address this notion of white privilege.

However, the issue is far deeper than the surface of the sometimes violent and vitriolic reactions from all sides of the conflict. The proverbial *two sides of every story* approach needs to be applied to this situation. As much as slavery, segregation and racism have split the nation, the abolition of the same has often created the same reactive affect. Even into the 21st century, although a black man occupied the Oval Office for eight years, racism is still with us.

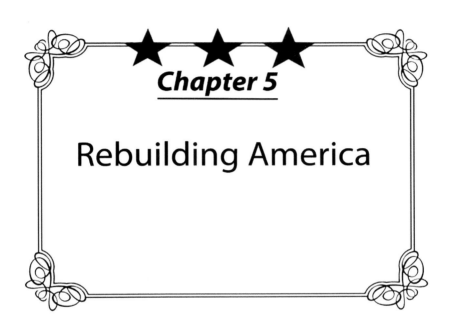

Chapter 5

Rebuilding America

CHAPTER FIVE

REBUILDING AMERICA

During the 2016 United States presidential election, there was much discussion regarding "building a wall of protection" for America. As in the years following 9/11 and in the Bible accounts, as human leaders debated about building walls with human effort, the people of God turned to prayer.

Often, human discussions and efforts to build or rebuild walls of brick and mortar are indicative of a greater need for spiritual fortification. Using the Book of Nehemiah as a pattern, let us consider what rebuilding America could look like. As we begin this process, let's review some interesting historical facts.

In the Hebrew Bible, the books of Ezra and Nehemiah are combined. In the manner of New Testament history, there are four Gospel accounts—Matthew, Mark, Luke and John, which all occurred during the same time period; and so it is with Ezra, Nehemiah, as well as Esther.

Ezra, Nehemiah, and Esther all come out of the same general period of Israel's history. They appear in our Christian Bibles in reverse order of the chronological order in which they took place. In other words, Esther actually happened when God first began to move in the midst of Israel's captivity to return Israel as a nation to the land.

God raised Esther, a Jew, to become the bride and queen of King Ahasuerus of Persia, who is also Artaxerxes, in the opening chapters of Nehemiah. By divine intervention, the king gave the command for Nehemiah to return to Jerusalem to build up the walls of the city which had been torn down by enemies.

From her throne in Persia, by God's grace, Esther influenced her husband, the king, to allow Nehemiah, his cupbearer, to return to Jerusalem. Nehemiah began the work of rebuilding the city of Jerusalem. Some twenty-five years later, Zerubbabel returned with about fifty thousand of the captives from Babylon, as is recorded in the book of Ezra.[1]

Artaxerxes and Ahasuerus are not names of the king, but rather respective titles meaning "the great king" and "the venerable father." As a sidebar, this is why Darius, the Mede, in Daniel's dispensation, had the same titles which also were not his name.

In examining the Bible formula for returning to God, we can look to Ezra, Nehemiah and Esther collectively:

1. The book of Ezra begins with the building of the temple. The restoration of the house of God is always the first thing in the way back to God.
2. Next, in Nehemiah comes with the rebuilding, or in our case—the building of the walls and the repairing of the gates. The building of the walls with secure gates represents *the meeting the need for security and strength*. Once the wall is built or rebuilt, the gates have to be installed or repaired. Thereafter, gatekeepers as well as watchmen on the wall, are assigned or reinstated.

What is the significance of having a city or a nation with a wall and gates—what does it symbolize? Once, one of the most famous landmarks in the world was the Berlin Wall, dividing the city in two. Today, people still travel to Israel to pray at the Wailing Wall. Ordinarily, though, a wall symbolizes *strength and protection*. In ancient cities, the only real means of defense were the gated walls. Sometimes these walls were tremendously thick and high. The walls of the city of Babylon, as recounted in the story of Daniel, were some 380 feet thick and over 100 feet high massive, tremendous walls. Therefore, the city of Babylon considered itself very safe.

There has been much talk and dissension in the 21st century regarding "building a wall" around the borders of the United States. There are those who believe that it is even more important to build up the spiritual defenses of America. In the final analysis, in order to build a strong America, this nation must first return to God.

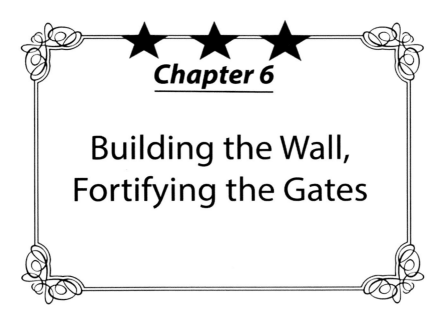

Chapter 6

Building the Wall, Fortifying the Gates

CHAPTER SIX

BUILDING THE WALL,
FORTIFYING THE GATES

As we consider the possibility of building both a spiritual wall for America and a physical wall with gates around her borders, we must consider the full process of rebuilding the wall and restoring the gates as in the Books of Ezra and Nehemiah. Ray Stedman's book *Nehemiah: Rebuilding the Walls,* was published in 1965, and remains a valuable reference and resource for developing strategies for building and rebuilding nations.

In Jerusalem, once the temple had been restored and the repairs to the wall had begun, Sanballat the Horonite and Tobiah the Ammonite servant heard about it, and this displeased them greatly that someone had come to seek the welfare of the people of Israel.

When Nehemiah and his company were rebuilding the city, there was an order to the process. We would do well to operate in these days according to the pattern of the Word of God.

Hebrews 8:5 (NKJV), "See that you make all things according to the pattern shown you on the mountain."

Abba Father God, Lord Jesus and Holy Spirit must be our answers to every need! There is much to be learned for today's battle in the books of Ezra, Nehemiah and Esther. Let us continue the journey in Nehemiah 3:32 to glean wisdom for the strategic process together:

First, they rebuilt the Sheep Gate (recovering the sheep of the Shepherd of Psalm 23 for this present season).

Then, they rebuilt the Fish Gate (for the fishers of men in Matthew 4:19 and Mark 1:17).

Next, they rebuilt the Gate of Yeshanah (the Old City, representing biblical foundations).

After that, the Dung Gate was repaired (this is self-explanatory; flush the waste, take out the trash).

Then, it's on to repair and open the Fountain Gate (the flow of Holy Spirit, the washing of the Word and the cleansing of the blood of Jesus.)

Next, repair the Pool of Shelah (which means being sent [lead] by the Spirit of God).

Move into the King's Garden (where we should find the fruit of the Spirit of Galatians in manifestation in the saints).

Then go on to the artificial (man-made) pool (as in man-made solutions such as grants, stimulus plans, etc., which are not all bad, but are not to be relied upon, simply used as we are led by Holy Spirit).

Next, repair the houses of the Mighty (prayer warriors and worshippers) Men (and women, since in the spirit there are no male and female, bond or free, only Christ, Lord of all).

Then we repair the districts—under the guidance of the apostles, prophets, evangelists, pastors and teachers, and the ministry gifts assigned to local church bodies in their dominion territories.

Then, there are the branch ministries, supported by the Armory (spiritual warfare), which through prayer buttresses the next door.

The Door of the High Priest (here prayer is a buttress or support and reinforcement for the work of the ministry of the saints of God)—the imagery and reality of prayer supporting and leading up to the next door. The Door of the High Priest is very profound! The path here leads around to the community of the saints devoted to serving the Lord.

The Houses of the Servants of Abba lead to the tower.

The Tower of the Court of the Guard (prayer watches) is occupied continually!

Then there is repair of the Water Gate (living water that Jesus speaks of in John 4:10-11, 7:38 and Revelations 7:17)—with the water being brought in daily, hourly and breath-by-breath through the labor of prayer! Often in Nehemiah's and Ezra's time, it was the women who carried the water because the men were so encumbered with worldly affairs during the day. Yet the hour is here now where all must worship Abba in spirit and in truth (John 4:23-24). For me, this revelation coincides with 2 Chronicles 7:14, "If my people, which are called by my name, shall humble themselves, and pray, and seek my face, and turn from their wicked ways; then will I hear from heaven, and will forgive their sin, and will heal their land."

From the Water Gate, we go on to the next gate.

The Horse Gate (jobs, promotions, prosperity, etc.) to every house and every chamber. All of this process affects the restoration of the House of the Temple Servants.

Finally, we arrive at the Muster Gate, which means the inspection or judgment gate; and for some the prison gate; but for many the victory gate.

We can conclude from this section of study that spiritual understanding is a necessary component to the rebuilding of a nation. As America returns to God, what an opportunity for healing and restoration this process brings for spirit, soul and body!

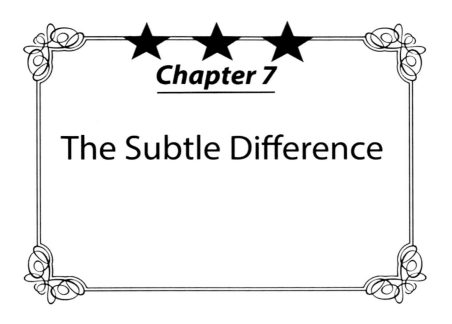

Chapter 7

The Subtle Difference

CHAPTER SEVEN

THE SUBTLE DIFFERENCE

"Then answered I them, and said unto them, The God of heaven, he will prosper us; therefore, we his servants will arise and build: but ye have no portion, nor right, nor memorial, in Jerusalem." (Nehemiah 2:20 KJV)

There is such a subtle difference in the expression of the intent to rebuild from Nehemiah and his team in his era, and the President of the United States of America and his associates in the 21st century in the aftermath of 9/11. Nehemiah called upon the God of Heaven as his source and resource. The inscription in the wall at Ground Zero in New York boasts no such acknowledgement of God.

Men like Ezra and Nehemiah realized that they could accomplish nothing on their own. Indeed, in John 5:19 and 30, the Lord Jesus says that He can do nothing of Himself. He goes on in John 15:5 to reveal Himself as the Vine and us as the branches.

The main take away from this study should be that the main strategy that is needed today is much prayer and devotion to Abba, our mighty Father, Creator God! Nehemiah was wise to set the workers to laboring with one hand and doing spiritual warfare with the other hand; while half worked, half prayed nonstop! (see Nehemiah 5:6).

The thing is today, while many are going around to town hall meetings, screaming and yelling, bringing about envy and strife and every evil work (James 3:14), we, as the Body of Christ, are called to prayer and worship—where we will find answers and strength for victory. Yes, we can go to a town hall meeting, but we must go in the love and grace of God, and pray and trust Him to open hearts so that people will hear Him in this hour!

Yes, our Kingdom work today includes restoring, reviving and feeding the sheep (people of God), catching the fish (the lost souls in the world) through evangelism and salvation for the lost, and reinforcing biblical foundations (though mature Christians need milk and meat, the new Christians need to know the foundations, and we can all use the Word). Once people are restored, revived, saved and taught, the dung (waste, sin, etc.) needs to be carted out of the Kingdom. Onto the Fountain, the leading or sending of the Holy Spirit, the King's Garden, artificial man-made solutions, the rising of the mighty warriors, establishing prayer and service districts, prayer buttress at the "Door of the High Priest" — our homes, the prayer tower, prayer watches, and then to the Horse Gate, or our jobs and our prosperity, from which we tithe and give for the Kingdom; and we are blessed and healed and full of joy!

Today, in our nation and across the globe, we are threatened by concepts and forces that would like to advance abortion, the destruction of the biblical model for marriage and family, the euthanasia of the elderly and infirm, racism, poverty, crime, famine, drought, and a crashing economy. Surely we don't need to rehearse the list.

I will share my own testimony (in the next chapter) of being healed from secret abortions. It is my testimony of being healed after the destruction of abortion on my own life and the lives of my preborn children. Being a victim of the population control genocide eugenics campaign, that is still prevalent today, gives me a personal connection to the pro-life movement. This testimony has led me to ask the question: "How can the *Dream* survive if we murder our children?"

Every aborted baby is like a slave in the womb of his or her mother. In the hands of the mother is the fate of that child—whether the child lives or dies—a decision given to the mother by Roe v. Wade. That choice, the final choice of whether the child lives or dies, should be left to God, who ultimately says, "Choose life!"

Acts 17:26 teaches us that we are one human race, designed and created of "one blood." If we want to see another race of people, we will have to look to Star Trek! "And He has made from one blood every nation of men to dwell on all the face of the earth, and has determined their pre-appointed times and the boundaries of their dwellings…" (Acts 17:26 NKJV).

Little babies in the womb and their parents (both mothers and fathers) are all human beings, regardless of ethnicity, age, gender, or physical fitness or lack thereof. We must regard and respect all human life in every circumstance.

My uncle, Dr. Martin Luther King, Jr., once said: "The next thing we must be concerned about, if we are to have peace on earth and good will toward men, is the nonviolent affirmation of the sacredness of all human life. ...Man is a child of God, made in His image, and therefore must be respected as such. ...And when we truly believe in the sacredness of human personality, we won't exploit people, we won't trample over people with the iron feet of oppression, we won't kill anybody." —MLK 1967, Christmas Sermon.

I am so very glad that my parents chose life for me. While I regret my secret abortions, I will always be grateful for God's grace and forgiveness, the blood of Jesus and the comfort of Holy Spirit; all bring the assurance that I will be united with my whole family in Heaven one day.

100 Days of Nonviolence

On January 15, 2014, my cousin Elder Bernice King, CEO of the King Center in Atlanta, Georgia, called for "100 Days of Nonviolence" in honor of her father, my uncle, Dr. Martin Luther King, Jr. She called for a halt of violent use of guns, words (the tongue) and the fist. I joined her in this mandate, adding that abortion is one of the most violent acts committed against humanity, and urged a "cease fire" on the wombs of women and the lives of their babies. For me, efforts of this type are all a part of rebuilding our nation and our world and claiming souls for Christ.

I only mention this action here because as we were rebuilding the wall, there were several attacks from the media and contrasting messages that were designed to distract us and call us off of the wall.

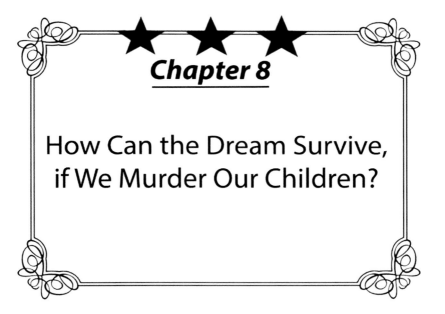

Chapter 8

How Can the Dream Survive, if We Murder Our Children?

CHAPTER EIGHT

HOW CAN THE DREAM SURVIVE IF WE MURDER OUR CHILDREN?

During the 20th century, the door was opened to invade the wombs of mothers, the stability of the family, the sanctity of marriage and the sacredness of the human personality. In the name of civil rights, abortion was legalized by the sanction of the Roe v. Wade case. Over 55 million babies have been legally aborted in America since then. Nearly one-third of those aborted babies are African Americans. Sadly, two of them are mine. As I reflect on the reality of black genocide that has loomed over the African American community since the days of slavery in this nation, I find that the dream of Martin Luther King is continually threatened by the abortion of our children, and the injury to the wombs and health of their mothers.

Films such as *Maafa 21*, *Blood Money*, and others provide pertinent data and evidence of a continuing pattern of genocide and eugenics, all rooted in the triple evils of racism, reproductive genocide and sexual perversion—a three-headed monster. This pattern must be broken by the power of truth— the power of God. It is my prayer that my personal testimony will shed light and broadcast liberating truth regarding the issue of abortion which pervades the civil rights of our weakest—the children in the wombs of vulnerable mothers.

"The next thing we must be concerned about if we are to have peace on earth and good will toward men is the nonviolent affirmation of the sacredness of all human life. ...Man is a child of God, made in His image, and therefore must be respected as such... And when we truly believe in the sacredness of human personality, we won't exploit people, we won't trample over people with the iron feet of oppression, we won't kill anybody." (MLK 1967 Christmas Sermon).

In this great country of ours, no one should be forced to pray or read any religious documents, and a woman should have the right to decide what to do with her own body. Thank God for the United States Constitution. That constitution, though, guarantees freedom of religion, not freedom from religion. The so-called doctrine of "separation of church and state" is not in our constitution. Nothing in our constitution forbids the free exercise of religion in the public square. Inherent in our constitutional right to "life, liberty and the pursuit of happiness," is the right to know the serious consequences of making a decision to deny religious freedom, or to abort our children.

Oh God, what would Martin Luther King, Jr. (who dreamed of having his four children judged by the content of their characters—not just by the color of their skin), do if he'd lived to see the contents of thousands of children's skulls emptied into the bottomless caverns of the abortionists pits? What would he say about the rivers of blood of the children cut down in gang wars and other dark deeds?

It is time for America, perhaps the most blessed nation on earth, to lead the world in repentance and in restoration of life! If only we can carry the freedom of repentance to its fullest potential. If only America can repent and turn away from the sins of our nation. We must allow light and life back into our lives!

Today, I live with a repentant heart and I pray in thanks each day for the Lord's forgiveness and blessing. I am a mother of six living children and a grandmother. Regretfully, I am also a post-abortive mother. I offer a tearful prayer that my sharing the tragedy of my life-altering experiences will help save the life of a child yet unborn.

My Testimony

In the early 1970's, even though some black voices were protesting against forced sterilization, artificial chemical birth control methods and abortion, there were many who were fooled and misled by propaganda that promoted such strategies. I was among those who were duped. As a result, I suffered one involuntary and one voluntary "legal" abortion.

My involuntary abortion was performed just prior to the passage of Roe v. Wade by my private pro-abortion physician without my consent. I had gone to the doctor to ask why my cycle had not resumed after the birth of my son. I did not ask for and did not want an abortion. The doctor said, "You don't need to be pregnant, let's see." He proceeded to perform a painful examination which resulted in a gush of blood and tissue emanating from my womb. He explained that he had performed an abortion called a "local D and C."

Soon after the Roe v. Wade decision, I became pregnant again. There was adverse pressure and threat of violence from the baby's father. The ease and convenience provided through Roe v. Wade made it too easy for me to make the fateful and fatal decision to abort our child. I went to a Planned Parenthood sanctioned doctor and was advised that the procedure would hurt no more than "having a tooth removed."

The next day, I was admitted to the hospital, and our baby was aborted. My medical insurance paid for the procedure. As soon as I woke up, I knew that something was very wrong. I felt very ill, and very empty. I tried to talk to the doctor and nurses about it. They assured me that "it will all go away in a few days. You will be fine." They lied.

Over the next few years, I experienced medical problems. I had trouble bonding with my son, and his five siblings who were born after the abortions. I began to suffer from eating disorders, depression, nightmares, sexual dysfunctions, and a host of other issues related to the abortion that I chose to have. I felt angry about both the involuntary and voluntary abortions, and very guilty about the abortion I chose to have. The guilt made me very ill. Like my uncle, Dr. Martin Luther King, Jr., who had received the Margaret Sanger Planned Parenthood Award in 1968, I became a victim of the lies of Planned Parenthood. They assured my uncle, they told me and millions of mothers and fathers that their agenda was to help our people. They lied. Their agenda is *deadly!*

I pray often for deliverance from the pain caused by my decision to abort my baby. I suffered the threat of cervical and breast cancer, and experienced the pain of empty arms after the baby was gone. Truly, for me and for countless abortive mothers, nothing on earth can fully restore what has been lost — only Jesus can.

My children have all suffered from knowing that they have a brother or sister that their mother chose to abort. Often, they ask if I ever thought about aborting them, and they have said, "You killed your baby." This is very painful for all of us. The aborted child's father also regrets the abortions. If it had not been for Roe v. Wade, I would never have had that second abortion.

My birthday is January 22, and each year this special day is marred by the fact that it is also the anniversary of Roe v.

Wade—and the anniversary of death for millions of babies. I and my deceased children are victims of abortion. The Roe v. Wade decision has adversely affected the lives of my entire family.

My grandfather, Dr. Martin Luther King, Sr., twice said, "No one is going to kill a child of mine." The first-time Daddy King said this was to my mother, who was facing an "inconvenient pregnancy" with me. The next time I was facing a pregnancy I told him about it. In both instances, Daddy King said no, and saved his lineage.

Tragically, two of his grandchildren had already been aborted when he saved the life of his next great-grandson with this statement. His son, Dr. Martin Luther King, Jr., once said, "The Negro cannot win as long as he is willing to sacrifice the lives of his children for immediate personal comfort and safety. Injustice anywhere is a threat to justice everywhere."

In light of Uncle Martin's pro-life stance, I find it extremely troubling that Planned Parenthood uses a ploy of publishing a speech Dr. King didn't write or deliver to pretend that Dr. King would have supported their agenda of death.

Dr. Martin Luther King, Jr. was pro-life, but his wife Coretta was pro-choice. Mrs. King attended the Planned Parenthood Award Ceremony in 1966, read a speech written by someone other than her husband, and accepted the Margaret Sanger Award in his name. Dr. Martin Luther King, Jr. did not attend the ceremony. He did not write the speech!

Like Mrs. Laura Bush, who in interviews and in her book, admits that she is pro-abortion, Mrs. Coretta Scott King was at odds with her husband's ideology regarding life and human sexuality. These women chose platforms that were not reconciled to the reality of the blessings of procreative reproductive health leading to monogamous healthy marriages between husbands and wives; the births of healthy babies; and the continuation of God's plan for families nurtured in love and righteousness.

It is ludicrous to suggest that Martin Luther King, Jr. would have endorsed any acts that chemically or surgically dismember and kill babies in the womb; butcher women under falsehood of providing "safe abortions"; and hide the truth that many hysterectomies, breast cancer surgeries and other "female reproductive illnesses" are the results of abortion. They promote death over life in the name of abortion and call it civil rights.

My uncle, Dr. Martin Luther King, Jr., could never have endorsed such tactics! This understanding leads me to ask this question:

How can the "Dream" survive if we murder our children? Every aborted baby is like a slave in the womb of his or her mother. In the hands of the mother is the fate of that child — whether the child lives or dies—a decision given to the mother by Roe v. Wade. That choice, the final choice of whether the child lives or dies, should be left to God, who ultimately says, "Choose life!"

I join the voices of thousands across America, who are SILENT NO MORE. We can no longer sit idly by and allow this horrible spirit of murder to cut down, yes cut out and cut away, our unborn and destroy the lives of our mothers. Our babies and our mothers must live!

I am very grateful to God for the spirit of repentance that is sweeping our land. In repentance, there is healing. In the name of Jesus, we must humble ourselves and pray, and turn from our wicked ways, so that God will hear from Heaven and heal our land.

I, like my uncle, Martin Luther King, Jr., have a dream. I still have a dream that someday the men and women of our nation, the boys and girls of America, will come to our senses, humble ourselves before God Almighty, and receive His healing grace. I pray that this is the day and the hour of our deliverance. I pray that we will regain a covenant of life and finally obtain the promised liberty, justice, and pursuit of happiness for all.

Let us end injustice anywhere by championing justice everywhere, including in the womb. May God, by His grace, have mercy on us all.

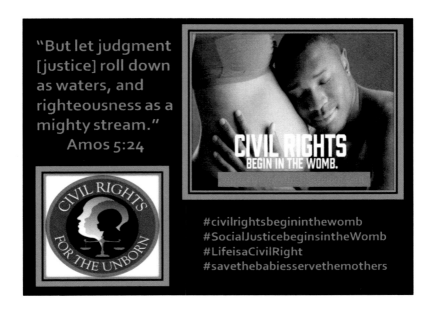

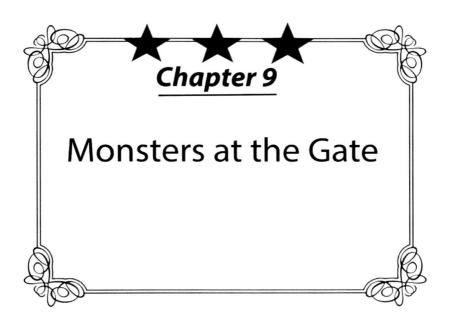

Chapter 9

Monsters at the Gate

CHAPTER NINE

MONSTERS AT THE GATES

In the books of Esther, Ezra and Nehemiah, we see that they battled with not only human foes, but with spiritual darkness. The same is the case in the 21st century. Esther had her Haman, Nehemiah had his Sanballat and Tobias, and Ezra dealt with the issue of carnality of the flesh.

If it is allowable, let us examine some passages from the book of Esther through 21st century lenses, comparing the conversation between Haman and the king, with the relationship of President Obama and Planned Parenthood:

And Planned Parenthood said to President Obama, "There are certain people known as evangelicals and other religious fanatics scattered and separated among the peoples in all of the United States under your administration; their laws are different from the common law of every other people in this nation and around the world; and they do not agree with the common laws of your Supreme Court and other decrees from your administration; Therefore, it is not appropriate for you, Mr. President, to tolerate them."

Planned Parenthood said to the President, "We need at least a million of U.S. tax dollars a day to help us deal with this. Issue an executive order that will fill our coffers. We will also use our great fortunes to ally this effort." The President agreed with Planned Parenthood, assigning edicts and orders to further the efforts. He added, "Take the money and do what you will to abort the dreams of the naysayers."

This message goes out to the faithful in the 21ˢᵗ century who would turn away from the struggle: "For if indeed you keep silent at this time, relief and deliverance will arise for the oppressed from another place, and yet you and your dreams will perish. Who knows? Perhaps you have come to a royal position for a time such as this?"

Do you recognize this Scripture passage? Read their source of inspiration in the book of Esther:

"And Haman said to King Ahasuerus, 'There is a certain people scattered and separated among the peoples in all of the provinces of your kingdom; their laws are different from every other people, and they do not observe the laws of the king; it is not appropriate for the king to tolerate them. If it pleases the king, let a decree be issued to destroy them, and I will pay ten thousand talents of silver to those who do the job, to bring to the treasury of the king. 'So the king removed his signet ring from his hand and gave it to Haman son of Hammedatha the Agagite, the enemy of the Jews. And the king said to Haman, 'The money is given to you and to the people to do with it as you see fit.'" (Esther 3:8-11 LEB)

"For if indeed you keep silent at this time, relief and deliverance will arise for the Jews from another place, and you and the family of your father will perish. Who knows? Perhaps you have come to a royal position for a time such as this." (Esther 4:14 LEB)

Do you recognize the correlation among the passages? The enemy is forever at the gates. It is always up to the believers to trust God and resist the enemy.

Issues such as genocide, infanticide, gendercide, abortion, euthanasia and all manner of inhumanity to man have plagued nations and civilizations throughout the ages. Human rights questions, civil rights questions, and religious rights questions continue to divide the hearts of humanity.

While only three such issues—racism, reproductive genocide and sexual perversion—have been chosen for in-depth discussion in this book, it is no way intended that the reader should consider them to the be the only challenges a nation must face when turning back to God. Divine social justice is a concept that is often rejected because such justice is grounded in the righteousness of God.

Indeed, there are monsters at the gates. Humble prayers and obedience to our Creator will keep them at bay and bring deliverance to our nation. This passage in Ephesians 6 is an essential battery in the arsenal of holy warriors as we pray to turn our nation back to God.

Ephesians 6 (KJV): "Children, obey your parents in the Lord: for this is right. Honour thy father and mother; which is the first commandment with promise; ³ That it may be well with thee, and thou mayest live long on the earth. And, ye fathers, provoke not your children to wrath: but bring them up in the nurture and admonition of the Lord. Servants, be obedient to them that are your masters according to the flesh, with fear and trembling, in singleness of your heart, as unto Christ; Not with eye service, as men pleasers; but as the servants of Christ, doing the will of God from the heart; With good will doing service, as to the Lord, and not to men: Knowing that whatsoever good thing any man doeth, the same shall he receive of the Lord, whether he be bond or free. And, ye masters, do the same things unto them, forbearing threatening: knowing that your Master also is in heaven; neither is there respect of persons with him."

"Finally, my brethren, be strong in the Lord, and in the power of his might. Put on the whole armour of God, that ye may be able to stand against the wiles of the devil. For we wrestle not against flesh and

blood, but against principalities, against powers, against the rulers of the darkness of this world, against spiritual wickedness in high places. Wherefore take unto you the whole armour of God, that ye may be able to withstand in the evil day, and having done all, to stand." "Stand therefore, having your loins girt about with truth, and having on the breastplate of righteousness; And your feet shod with the preparation of the Gospel of peace; Above all, taking the shield of faith, wherewith ye shall be able to quench all the fiery darts of the wicked. And take the helmet of salvation, and the sword of the Spirit, which is the word of God: Praying always with all prayer and supplication in the Spirit, and watching thereunto with all perseverance and supplication for all saints..."

Friends we are faced with a 3 headed monster that resists the Word of the Lord - "Be fruitful and multiply" (procreate)!

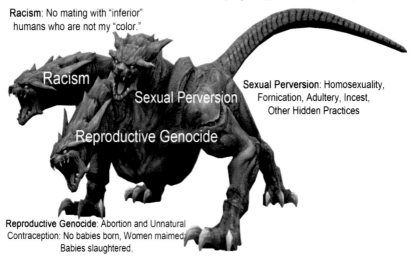

Racism: No mating with "inferior" humans who are not my "color."

Racism

Sexual Perversion

Sexual Perversion: Homosexuality, Fornication, Adultery, Incest, Other Hidden Practices

Reproductive Genocide

Reproductive Genocide: Abortion and Unnatural Contraception: No babies born, Women maimed; Babies slaughtered.

Human Sexuality:
And It All Started with an Apple!

This section is a series of emails, conversations, and research which took place between 2013-2015—compiled by Dr. Alveda C. King:

The growing controversies surrounding 1st Amendment religion and freedom of speech rights are reaching fever pitch. The following "discussion" springs forth from a series of current emails and communications in response to emails regarding Apple CEO, Folsom Street Fair, and Human Sexuality in General. (Some of this is touched on in my book *King Rules*, Chapter 4.)

Part One: Eunuchs and Sexual Confusion

Dearest "R" (initial of an email partner)—Several years ago, God "spoke" to me about human sexuality. Never mind that God had forgiven my many sins including abortion, gluttony, sexual misconduct and so much more. In a self-righteous rant, I (not God) was condemning "transgender" RuPaul to Hell. There I was, ranting and raving, at RuPaul on late night TV. Reaching fever pitch, I heard God's gentle yet rebuking voice: "I love RuPaul as much as I love you!"

Wow! I collapsed on the couch, shuddering and repenting as my spiritual sight came online. I saw RuPaul through the eyes of Christ, through Christ's compassionate blood-washed lenses! Thus began a new level of ministry for me. I write briefly of this in KING RULES –"Guard Your Heart."

You wrote that truly the Body of Christ has done much harm to the flock of God's creation who are dealing with sexu issues. To be honest, every human being has issues; and God isn't desiring to write anyone off. That's why He gave us Jesus (see John 3:16-17).

"Do you think that I like to see wicked people die? says the Sovereign LORD. Of course not! I want them to turn from their wicked ways and live." (Ezekiel 18:23 NLT)

See? It's true! God loves everyone and wants us with Him forever. We all just need to be "cleaned up."

Now, with everyone "being born into sin," people can be born with all types of issues and conditions, including sexual issues. There are reasons for this: heredity, birth and after birth (and after the FALL) negative impacts, etc.

Jesus even explained some of this in Matthew 19:11-12 (NLT), "Not everyone can accept this statement…only those whom God helps. Some are born as eunuchs, some have been made eunuchs by others, and some choose not to marry for the sake of the Kingdom of Heaven. Let anyone accept this who can."

There are at least three different groups of people who were defined as *Eunuchs* in biblical times:

A eunuch specifically was a male who would not have sex with a woman (and in some cases no sex at all).

1. There was the eunuch who would not have sex for religious purposes and entered a monastery.
2. There was the eunuch who was castrated to work in harems.
3. There was the (male) eunuch who was born with feminine traits and had no sexual interest in women.

(Note: "Born that way"): Remember Jesus confirmed this in the New Testament. The problem is, people think Jesus was condoning this situation. Actually, Jesus wasn't. He was simply explaining it. The whole chapter pretty much deals with human sexuality by the way.)

Important to know—God didn't design homosexuality. The meddling Usurper (Satan) stole the keys to the laboratory, made *knockoffs* and goofed up perfection. He tried to make the unnatural a natural thing. Don't blame God!

Ancient Eunuchs and Roman Law

The Eunuch who would not have sex because of religion was not covered under Roman law. In ancient Roman Law, it is laid out by the Roman jurist Ulpian in a document known as *Lex Julia et Papia, Book 1* (Digest 50.16.128). "Eunuch is a general designation: the term includes those who are eunuchs by nature, as well as those who are mutilated."[1]

The Law

The law (Digest 28.2.6) says that someone who cannot easily procreate is nonetheless entitled to institute a posthumous heir, but it gives no concrete examples of such a man.[1]

Also the jurist Ulpian refers to the non-castrated man as a eunuch and refers to the castrated as castrated men.

Eunuchs Who Were Born as Such Could Marry and Adopt Children

Eunuchs from birth who were freemen, unlike mutilated eunuchs, were eligible for marriage and for adopting children: (Digest 23.3.39.1, 28.2.6).[1]

In fact, anatomically "whole eunuchs" had all the rights and duties of ordinary men.

The term *eunuchs from birth* means nothing was missing. Consequently, they were physically sexually unimpaired. Anatomically these were not people who had missing genitalia; or something rarer, having been born with both male and female genitalia. They were physically whole, but they would not have sex with women.

From birth, eunuchs were homosexual men of that time and had all rights and duties of ordinary men. Today, we refer to them as "gay men." There isn't much research about from birth, female eunuchs. Yet research supports the possibility that design tampering has resulted in some females being born this way. However, lack of study, knowledge and understanding could lead someone to believe that some homosexual people are lying when they say they were born that way.

A perfect example appears in the television series *Empire*. One of the characters is homosexual. Even as a very little boy, he liked to wear his mother's high heels and scarves and mimic the way she walked with hands on hips. His mother remained sympathetic throughout his childhood and adult years. On the other hand, his father abhorred his son's sexuality, and even stuffed him in a garbage can, in an alley, wearing his mother's clothes in a flashback scene.

Metaphorically speaking, what is difficult to have people understand is that God did not create this confusion. The problem is that when the Usurper stole the lab keys and goofed up the design, he amplified lust and smudged sexual desire when he goofed up the design. He resented the procreative gene and deflected it with lust. How cruel!

Sexual Confusion: "Worse followed. Refusing to know God, they soon didn't know how to be human either—women didn't know how to be women, men didn't know how to be men. Sexually confused, they abused and defiled one another, women with women, men with men—all lust, no love. And then they paid for it, oh, how they paid for it—emptied of God and love, godless and loveless wretches." (Romans 1:26-27 MSG)

Yes, Usurper's plan causes confusion and lack of proper enjoyment of Creator's design. This obviously ticks off the Creator. God creates *procreative love*. The best the Usurper can come up with is a frustrated substitute.

Adding insult to injury, the Usurper stirs human trafficking, child abuse and molestation into the mix. Sometimes this brings about sexual confusion among the young, especially during the pre-puberty and puberty stages of life for boys and girls.

To complicate matters, the Usurper adds hybrid models into the system—people who have sex with everyone and everything. Wow! This is just as cruel as adding cancer, hypertension, heart attacks, depression and a lot more mess into his scheme; which by the way he does.

So is there any wonder why "gays" are searching for *agape love* and demanding answers to this mess that the Usurper created? (Whether they understand what's true or not, that GOD is not responsible for this confusion, everybody was created to be loved by GOD.)

Keep praying for understanding! Remember now: God did not make this mess! The Usurper did. God is good. The Usurper is evil and mean.

Part Two: God Isn't Schizophrenic

Dear "R," recently you wrote to me about the Folsom Street Fair (a type of homosexual celebration). About the same time, Apple CEO, Tim Cook, publicly shared his homosexual lifestyle. He basically said that his sexuality is a gift from God. Wow! So much is "coming out of the closet" isn't it?

The thing is, God isn't schizophrenic. For instance, God wouldn't design and create a sick body and then send Jesus to heal that person. So it stands to reason that God would not make, as in design, and create a homosexual person and then command the person not to be homosexual. I understand the confusion and misguided responses from those with this issue.

Knowing, believing, or at least hoping or thinking that God created humans and that God is good, they mistakenly accepted the lie that the Bible is wrong and that somehow the Word of God is either a lie or a mistake. It is truly amazing how many people will believe a lie before they will believe the truth.

Well, there is a lie. There is a mistake. Over at Apple, Mr. Cook will maybe even get this revelation: In the beginning, God, our awesome Creator, created, designed, copyrighted and trademarked us; male and female. God built us to procreate, to unite sexually as male combined with female, to "be fruitful and multiply."

Then, in perhaps the most notorious historical attempt at a corporate takeover, a counterfeit agent slipped into corporate headquarters—an executive suite, AKA *the Garden of Eden*, and proceeded to usurp trade secrets. The unsuspecting female executive partook of the bribe; her male counterpart was not exactly unaware but chose to remain loyal to his companion.

Thus began the *big lie*. The *counterfeit knockoff Usurper* was able to temporarily pollute the design, fashioning it to his own liking, and lacking the purity of the original.

The Usurper even went so far as to feign his own religion and philosophy to further alienate human beings from understanding the supernatural divine love connection. Known today as *secular humanism*, its disciples resist all knowledge of a supernatural God's sovereign desire to love us.

Secular humanism can be defined as *a religious worldview based on atheism, naturalism, evolution, and ethical relativism.* Theologically, secular humanists lean toward atheism. Philosophically, secular humanists are naturalists. The scientific beliefs of the secular humanists are closely aligned with their theological and philosophical beliefs: wherein, if there is no supernatural, then life, including human life, must be the result of a purely natural phenomenon. Hence, secular humanists must believe in evolution.

Warning: People will believe a lie before they believe the truth!

Thus, with each new lying modification of the Counterfeiter, in each generation, more and more glitches appeared in the models and design, including sicknesses, diseases, confusion; murder, and on and on and on. I've even heard some people say things like: "God must have wanted me to have cancer" or, "God made me sick." Does that make sense at all? God isn't mean. The Usurper is. Jesus is a healer, not a sadist!

Think about this. Convince women that sexual liberation includes taking shots, pills, surgeries, chemicals, etc. to alter their reproductive cycles. The water supplies in the cities get flooded with the overflow of estrogen and hormones that are eliminated and flushed in the bathrooms. Testosterone and estrogen levels go screwy, and bingo, more sexual confusion.

Alert: Creator God has to make zip, zero, absolutely no modifications to the original male and female model and purpose of the man (male and female) species.

Now, in the beginning, Creator, God made a perfect design—man. The prototype Adam (which translates as "mankind" or humankind in original Hebrew), was male and female combined. Then, in the creative process, in compassion and love, Creator God did a brilliant design improvement. He made two of the one, then rejoined them in holy matrimony, and gave them the gift to sexually procreate! Wow!

In comes the Usurper who steals the lab keys and messes it all up. How sad and mean. To make matters worse, the counterfeit models are plagued with so many other viral issues like adultery, fornication, child molestation and abuse, burning lust, subsequent mental and physical attacks, and on and on. Truly, the counterfeit models that war against the original procreative design are fraught with issues.

"R" please read this email note from my friend MT:

Darling, these are my sentiments as well. The Lord showed me that those with this "hijacked propensity" for loving God are more able to transcend the heterosexual boundaries "spiritually" meaning that the homosexual and transgender etc., man's ability to give himself HOLYstically body soul and spirit to God, does not have the same obstacles that a heterosexual man does.

It's also a matter of *identity theft*; the power of generational sin to warp the human body as well. ...A lot to it, but, "Love is a mega key," as you said.

I once told a gay man that the reason he felt as he did was that God had given him a special gift to love his son in a deeper way—the spirit of perversion had then driven him to interpret this and play it out, in a physical way. The following week, he broke up with his lover.

I'm inclined to believe the "trans" thing is a propensity and ability to embrace the divine masculine and divine feminine, which the defeated loser has skewed. (He is a terrible spoilsport!) Blessings darling... I'm sure Abba will mega use your Godly insights!

Love, MT (end of MT's email response)

Alveda's response to MT: By the way MT, by design, complete expression in the harmonious sexual act between a male and female releases certain emissions, which are separate and distinct semen from male and arousal fluid from the woman, as well as certain endorphins and hormonal releases specific to each gender which allow sexual fulfillment. These are scientifically absent in same sex encounters, often resulting in unquenched burning lust at the end of the sexual encounter.

Alveda King continues her email conversation to "R":

"R" if we would simply consider that all people want to be loved and accepted, and that the Bible says that the unlovely deserve more of our compassion and attention than those that we consider to be lovely, then we can say why people work so hard to "normalize" or at least "marginalize" negative responses to issues, traits and behaviors that are often deemed unsuitable. This is true for many areas of life and is not confined to sexuality.

Understanding this, we might even be able to agree that sin can result in attacks on the dignity of human beings, bringing in close association the guilt and shame that accompany, and follow certain actions and behaviors. Then we might even understand why people fight to pass laws to force others to accept various issues, traits and behaviors. Sadly, acceptance doesn't correct the problems associated with the issues. Much of what is wrong is systemic, stemming from certain dysfunctions of human families.

Along with this insight come the problems resulting from imbalances of single parents' homes (with the lack of either mothers or fathers). Children need the modeling of both the male and female as they are being raised. Furthermore, parents having a boy may want a girl or vice versa. The baby in the womb, hearing or sensing gender rejection, may be impacted.

As another example, a boy raised by a mother who braids and puts pink ribbons in his hair may end up with some gender confusion, trying to be like a girl to please his mother. Or a girl who wants to please her father who has only daughters may model "boyish" behaviors to please her father. It's all out there.

So now what? Hating each other isn't going to fix this. Neither are witch hunts. Creator God is or has worked it all out: A way to be born again! Rather than scratch the entire project, Creator God first introduced a global flood, and later a cleansing agent; an anecdote; a transforming serum—AKA the blood of Christ. Good news: No more floods! The powerful blood serum is available.

So the solution is *the promise of God*. The mistake is believing that God ever designed poverty, sickness, abortion, sexual confusion—every sin known to human—and death.

For example, God didn't make me fat any more than God makes people gay. All of this is the Usurper's design!

Self-righteous religious zealots, who teach only about the wages of sin without promoting the loving gift of *eternal life from God*, need to stop it!

"R," I'm so glad you are speaking and teaching of God's love and gifts, which include no condemnation in Jesus Christ. The law of the spirit of life in Christ Jesus makes us free!

Friends, why spend your soul on buying the knockoff when you can have the real thing? (end of "R" email conversations)

Part Three: God's Design

As humans, we are all born into sin. That's not God's fault. Sin is a byproduct of the knockoff that happened in the Garden. An "apple" was reportedly involved.

Now I'm thinking that we should thank God for modern technology that allows us to communicate in such a way as to overcome evil with good. Please tell Mr. Cook that I won't be boycotting him or Apple. Instead, I'll thank God for the wisdom to use technology for His glory, no matter which humans put upgrades on the market. This biblical position includes defending procreative marriage, decrying abortion, defending life and several other Bible-based standards. Yet, this can be done the way Jesus is leading us.

God bless Mr. Tim Cook, and those partaking in the Folsom Street Fair, and every soul who has been bruised and tricked by the Counterfeiter. Once they see the truth, they may even want to "go and sin no more."

This once hidden, now revealed conceptual thought centers on Matthew 19:11-12, as it relates to eunuchs who are eunuchs because they are born with no desire for sexual relations with women.

In context, first note Jesus' teaching on marriage from Matthew 19:10-12 (MSG) as follows:

Jesus' disciples objected, "If those are the terms of marriage, we're stuck. Why get married?" But Jesus said, "Not everyone is mature enough to live a married life. It requires a certain aptitude and grace. Marriage isn't for everyone. Some, from birth seemingly, never give marriage a thought. Others never get asked—or accepted. And some decide not to get married for Kingdom reasons. But if you're capable of growing into the largeness of marriage, do it."

While Jesus seems to agree that marriage may not be for everyone, He qualifies the acknowledgment by explaining that although it very well may be more advantageous to remain unmarried (as Paul chose to and as Jesus chose to), only a few men are capable of living sexually separate from women because exclusive, permanent, agape-driven, sexual union with *one* woman is God's design for nearly all men.

The exception to this are eunuchs who have no desire for women because they: (1) were forcibly neutered; (2) choose (by God's special grace) to remain celibate for religious purposes; or (3) are born without desire for sexual union with women.

Of the three categories, only category (2) is by God's design. Category (1) is obviously the result of evil decisions by oppressors. I believe that that category (3) is a broad category that covers all those who were born without natural sexual desire through some coding error in their DNA, as a result of sin and the Fall.

Some of these men (and women) are born (not created as such by God) with classic genetic disorders such as Klinefelter Syndrome or Turner Syndrome; some suffer from insufficient hormonal production so that sexual desire and potency do not fully manifest; some are born with psychological issues like severe autism that makes intimacy of any kind undesirable; and yes, some have an atypical balance of hormones or brain abnormalities that predispose them to desire the same sex/gender.

Yet, none of these category (3) results are by God's design. They are all a result of genetic errors, like the chemical imbalances in the brain that drive some people to seek the dopamine-enhancing effects of certain drugs, or the chronically low leptin levels that some people experience that make overeating a constant temptation, etc.

All of the above leads to the question: "Why did God design humankind as male and female anyway?" Seriously. He could have made us genderless and caused us to procreate asexually like whiptail lizards. Why didn't He?

The answer becomes clear when we realize that God is *Agape*. Agape is defined by the indefatigable impetus to reach outside of itself and elevate something other than itself or its own image to the highest place of value. God was perfect in eternity without the need for anyone or anything else. The fellowship and love between Father, Son, and Holy Ghost were all sufficient for *all* of God's needs. Yet, out of the Godhead arose (and continually arises) a desire and passion to pour Himself into another being, so that this other being may know the inexpressible joy of God's self-giving.

This is why we know that issues and behaviors such as racism, abortion, sexual confusion, poverty, sickness, murder—and every harm known to humans are not of God. So if you have been affected with any of the above, remember—you can be *born again*.

In the Old Testament, people were wiped out in the midst of their issues. People were stoned and cities were burned down for sexual sins. It is now a new day people! Even though the Bible, loaded with insight on human sexuality, people today are still perishing in their sins due to lack of knowledge. For instance, in Song of Solomon, down to nibbling lilies in the garden, is a powerful lesson on both agape and erotic love. By the way, does anyone really believe the male lover was eating flowers?

Today, we can discover in the New Testament, how Jesus, the Son of a God, introduced healing and deliverance with "Ye who is without sin…" and "Go and sin no more."

Yes, the pure, untainted blood of Jesus, pure unpolluted DNA which cannot die, is available. Why is this blood pure? It is untainted by human DNA from an earthly father. Jesus' supernatural birth exempted Him from DNA pollution by the Usurper. He was not "born into sin." So the superhuman blood of Jesus antidote is untainted. Weird but true. So, let's all get that antidote, why don't we?

After all, every human being is born into sin because of the corporate crimes of the Usurper who tainted our human blood during the *fall of humanity*. Now, because of the Creator's gift of Jesus, the Son of God, and His precious superhuman blood, we can be born again and transformed.

Can we transform ourselves? Nicodemus asked Jesus that a long while back. The answer remains the same. *No.*

Follow-up question: Can and will God help us? Yes! With the precious gifts of abiding faith, hope and love! Yes! The good news is that we can be born again!

Part Four: Agape Love is Never the Problem

In 2015, the U.S. Supreme Court used common human law and reasoning to attempt to rewrite Creator's plan. Mrs. Michelle Obama, Mrs. Hillary Clinton and Representative Debbie Wasserman Schultz said, "Love won" in the 2015 Supreme Court decision on same-sex marriage. Their allies in the LGBT movement have repeatedly asked, "How can love be unconstitutional?" Whether deliberate or not, this just serves to confuse the issue.

Love is not the problem. You can love who you want. It's the sex that is the problem. Sex is not the same as love. People get that mixed up even in marriage. Sex should be part of that marriage union, as that is where children come from. Of course, all the models we have today are broken. But that was the design. We have people all confused. How it got mixed up is a long story I can't go into here. It would take days, but we have a lot of teaching to do on this issue.

My dad, A.D. King, Uncle MLK, and Granddaddy King passed on to me their beliefs on biblical marriage. Life is a human and civil right; so is procreative marriage. Spiritually and biblically speaking, you can't put abortion and homosexual unions in the same category as blacks in the civil rights movement. Daddy, Uncle MLK and Granddaddy would never condone such attempts.

Go Back to the Beginning

We must now go back to the beginning, starting with Genesis, and teach about God's plan for marriage. Parents and families need to be teaching it too. Sexual abuse and improper touching were the problem when I was young but now the confusion is with who can marry who.

America and much of the world has lost God's perspective on the issue of marriage and that's why the U.S. Supreme Court was able to get away with ruling the way it did. Years of wrong teaching, or no teaching, preceded the ruling. It's time to start from scratch and lay the foundation all over again.

So what we need to look at is to *go back to the beginning* and the purpose of marriage and family and human sexuality—and how we can fix what got broken. When we began to abandon the Creator and the original plan, the original blueprint and went toward human design, that's when the problems began to occur. When you don't know the purpose of a thing—why and how something was designed—you will abuse it. And so we're getting away from the original plan and the original design.

Common Law vs. Natural Law

Confusion also reigns in deciphering the difference between common law and natural law. As a paralegal, an educator, and one who served two terms in the Georgia House in the 1970s and 1980s, I have studied the Bible, natural law, and human common law.

I even read the other day about a lawsuit for millions of dollars by a homosexual man against Bible publishers. He says that the Bible's references to homosexuality have caused him harm and pain. He thinks winning the money and attempting to shut down Bible publishers will make him feel better?

As to the Supreme Court, they're looking at the common law and man's design, but the natural law is God's law and God's design, and natural law will line up with that. So to me, theirs was a human common law decision. It is better to obey God's law, I am bound to do that, and of course my uncle Dr. King, my grandfather Daddy King, my Daddy A.D. King, would agree with me and many of my brothers and sisters in the clergy. Many of us have made a commitment to follow God's law.

Are we the final JUDGE? No. Do we mess up sometimes? Yes, and we can know that our Lord will be there to forgive us. Remember we will all be "held accountable" in the end. Every Christian, everyone, you don't have to be a Christian, will stand before God in the final judgment, but my Lord Jesus said, "No one comes to the Father except by Me," and I can expect mercy from my Father—that is the Christian perspective. We will stand before God but we will have an advocate. Only the atheist says, "There is no God."

The other mistake that many make—and I'm speaking now as a minister and author of several books on spiritual topics—is to misinterpret the nature of God. God is love, but that's not all God is. The fullness of God is *mercy and judgment* and they both exist in the final reality. We often don't model that well as Christians.

Of course, judgment works more than one way. The Bible teaches us to judge ourselves before we judge others. God judges us all. Some people consider reminders that sin is a problem a "judgment." Ignoring our own sins, while pointing to the sins of others, is hypocritical. Casting the first stone is bad. Pretending to be pious is bad. Self-examination is a primary factor in judging oneself. Jesus truly said to the accusers of the woman caught in the act, "You who are without sin, cast the first stone." Judgment is real, and as we return to God we can.

"For the time has come for judgment, and it must begin with God's household. And if judgment begins with us, what terrible fate awaits those who have never obeyed God's Good News?" (1 Peter 4:17 NLT)

Every time I judge myself, I find myself lacking. I have experienced two abortions, sexual trauma as a child, have had three husbands; yet now, like the woman at the well and woman caught in the act, I am forgiven. I've been divorced three times, and even today, I don't indulge in alcohol. I may have half a glass, or at communion, because I know I was once an alcoholic, so I don't indulge.

In the year 1983, I was born again and decided to follow and serve God; I became very transparent about my mistakes— alcoholism, fornication, and abortion. Before being born again, I thought those things were okay, and now that I know they're not okay, I will speak of the liberty and the joy that I have from *not* having to be fearful and hide from my sins.

Even with my children, when I first told them about things that I had done in my past, we had to pray and do a lot of healing. So when my children and I speak candidly, they're ready to avoid some of the pitfalls that I had experienced.

You have to *show* the transformation. I used to be like *this* and now I'm not; and how did I get to that *not*?

Identifying the "Author of Confusion"

As a licensed, ordained minister and an evangelist, I will not preside over a same-sex wedding. I also won't marry many who wish to say traditional vows. I have such an extensive counseling program that although couples keep coming to me, but they tend to drop out before we get to the altar. I don't want them to have to go through what I went through (with divorce).

Agape love is never a problem; it's the *eros* and the sex that can become a problem. The Usurper tries to hijack love. It's just confusion. The Bible clearly identifies the "author of confusion." It's the Devil. But we have to be watchful in our responses and not be hateful—that's where we fail as Christians. Love never fails, sometimes sex does.

Excerpt from a *Charisma Magazine* article by Linda Italiano, a woman who confessed Lesbianism to her pastor:

"Thankfully, I was wrong about all of this. I requested a meeting with the pastor where I told her everything and I was met with love and respect. I was also shown exactly what the Bible says about homosexuality and it was made clear to me that it was unacceptable and wrong. I came away from that meeting still feeling welcome and accepted in the church, but understanding that homosexuality is a sin like any other sin. I understood that the Word of God is more important than anything else, and He is the answer to all of my problems. It did not take very long before I was completely delivered from the homosexual lifestyle and I totally renounced it. God did for me what I had been unwilling or unable to do for myself."[2]

(Important Scripture references and additional research links regarding sexual sins including but not limited to homosexuality can be found in chapter End Notes[3].)

Part Five: And the Two Become One

From time to time, many have written about the reality of the one-flesh bond that comes into existence as a consequence of sexual intercourse and the spiritual legal constraints with regard to the formation of that bond.[4]

After the first one-flesh bond is formed, it remains in existence forever, and every time they have sex it gets stronger and stronger. The only way to break this bond is by way of a very special petition to Father, Yah. It is possible to pollute the bond when sexual intercourse occurs with other partners outside the bond.

As the one-flesh bond gets stronger and is uninterrupted by sexual liaisons with others, the two-people become more and more one. They start to know each other's thoughts, they start to share thoughts, they start to think alike and act alike until, with a very strong one-flesh bond, they become a powerfully united, spiritual force, and their prayers become extremely powerful — two in concert (perfect harmony). This phenomenon happens whether they are serving Father or not.

If in sexual union, the man and woman are serving Father, their prayers become more powerful as they become closer to one another and more one with each other; just as we become more powerful in our relationship with Father the more we become one with Him and become filled with His Spirit. In fact, the human man-woman one-flesh bond is given to us, so that we can better understand being one with Father.

Note that the one-flesh bond is formed in every sexual situation, so it is just as powerful for unbelievers as believers. For this reason, religious demonic spirits lie to believers and cause believers to have negative attitudes towards sex and sexuality with the objective of minimizing the strength of the one-flesh bond that believers share. The lies about the one-flesh bond also result in people having multiple inappropriate one-flesh bonds.

For believers, Father desires for us to have intensely passionate and fulfilling sex lives so that we can build strong and intense one-flesh bonds. There is nothing we can do sexually (that does not cause pain and harm to our bodies) *within holy matrimony* that is unacceptable to Father. It is numerous, random and illegitimate one-flesh bonds that Father hates and forbids.

The one-flesh bond, properly consummated and properly maintained between Christians, is a massively powerful thing, and a thing of great beauty. In addition to forming a one-flesh bond, sexual love-making gives rise to the creation (making) of love, in an intense spiritual force intended to bind the couple together

Every time you tell your covenant man or woman that you love them, you add a small amount to the love-bond that exists between them. The more you think of each other sexually and talk to each other sexually, the stronger the one-flesh bond and the love-bond becomes. The love-bond can be broken down by repeated arguments and anger but, apart from that, it cannot be cut off.

It is possible for a man and a woman to be separated by thousands of miles and yet grow closer and closer by virtue of their communication by way of thoughts, messages and spoken communication and by sexual climax thinking of one another.

Note that sex between men (man with man or woman with woman) is forbidden, as is sex with a woman who is one with another man. Both of these are adultery and an abomination in Father's sight because they result in one-flesh bonds between men. It is also an abomination for a believer to have sex and form a one-flesh bond with an unbeliever.

To sum it up for now, human sexuality was designed by God for one purpose. The primary divine purpose of human sexuality, and indeed all sexuality is procreation. There is a corresponding sexual drive that is compatible to the procreation plan. The primal drive is best served when participants use the divine prescription for sexuality.

The secondary gratuitous benefit of sexual interaction among the species is *pleasure*. After all, if sex didn't feel good, how many people would find the time to engage in the exchange? Challenges arise in the arena when there is a lack of understanding of purpose, and human greed and error.

Throughout the ages, God's plan for family and sexuality has been under attack. As a result, many people are just not fully aware of God's purpose for sex. And to be honest, there are some people who don't believe in God and don't care about a divine plan.

Rather than judge our fellow and sister human beings, we need to teach and pray with open hearts and compassionate truth. And when all else fails remember: GOD IS IN CHARGE. CREATOR'S LOVE NEVER FAILS.

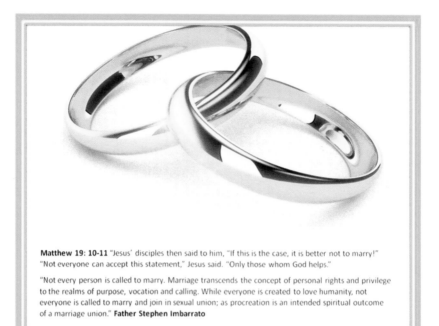

Matthew 19: 10-11 "Jesus' disciples then said to him, "If this is the case, it is better not to marry!" "Not everyone can accept this statement," Jesus said. "Only those whom God helps."

"Not every person is called to marry. Marriage transcends the concept of personal rights and privilege to the realms of purpose, vocation and calling. While everyone is created to love humanity, not everyone is called to marry and join in sexual union; as procreation is an intended spiritual outcome of a marriage union." **Father Stephen Imbarrato**

Chapter 10

Conclusion:
America's Return

CHAPTER TEN

CONCLUSION: AMERICA'S RETURN

As we set our hearts to return to God, we must be ever grateful to acknowledge the incredible sacrifice God made for us to become not only His creations, but we can become His children.

"So God created man in his own image, in the image of God he created them; male and female he created them." (Genesis 1:27 NIV)

"But to all who believed him [Jesus] and accepted him [as God's Son and our Lord], he gave the right to become children of God." (John 1:12 NLT)

As children of God, we have keys to His Kingdom, we have authority given to us by God's Son, Jesus Christ, and we are "more than conquers in Christ Jesus." We can speak to mountains and they will move.

Here in America, author and lecturer Lance Wallnau has introduced to us the "seven mountains of influence" over which we, as God's people, can influence for good. It is surely time to occupy until Jesus comes.

Just as this manuscript was about to hit the press, toward the end of 2016, a message that had been sparking in my heart emerged to take its place on the pages of this book. While I struggled with the title, wanting to call it "The Esther Moment Season" several scriptural themes flooded in all at once. I have a saying: "When peripherals collide, convergence is imminent." Well, here is the message as it appeared to me: *The Esther Moment Season.*

During a mid-morning Bible reading and meditation, while sitting alone with God, this word was revealed to me in Scriptures and understanding. While the passages in the messages are primarily centered on testimonies of biblical women, this is not a message solely for women. The themes of going forth and *sinning no more*, and embracing God's call on our lives is for everyone who will receive it:

> "...*For my house shall be called a house of prayer*
> *for all peoples." (Isaiah 56:7 ESV)*

In Isaiah 54:1, 4-10, 13-15, 17 (ESV), while God was ministering to the barren women and unwed mothers of Isaiah's day, the message is also to post-abortive, divorced, abused, rebellious and yes, barren women of the 21st century. What touched my heart the most (because I am divorced and post-abortive) were God's words to women who have suffered the pain of either never conceiving, having conceived or miscarried, or experienced the pain of raising children amidst broken families.

To the barren and childless: "For the children of the desolate one will be more than the children of her who is married," says the Lord. So many women have longed to birth children from their wombs and were not able to bear natural babies. Some drowned in the bitterness of the loss; yet God has blessed many others to adopt, mentor, pastor and nurture children of the spirit.

To the desolate women, who have lost either children or their dreams: "For the children of the desolate one will be more than the children of her who is married," says the Lord, who has compassion on you. The Lord has not forgotten us; He has not forsaken us.

The Promise in these passages: "All your children shall be taught by the Lord, and great shall be the peace of your children. In righteousness you shall be established; you shall be far from oppression, for you shall not fear; and from terror, for it shall not come near you. If anyone stirs up strife, it is not from me; whoever stirs up strife with you shall fall because of you."

"Sing, O barren one, who did not bear; break forth into singing and cry aloud, you who have not been in labor! For the children of the desolate one will be more than the children of her who is married," says the Lord.

"Fear not, for you will not be ashamed; be not confounded, for you will not be disgraced; for you will forget the shame of your youth, and the reproach of your widowhood you will remember no more. For your Maker is your husband, the Lord of hosts is his name; and the Holy One of Israel is your Redeemer, the God of the whole earth he is called. For the Lord has called you like a wife deserted and grieved in spirit, like a wife of youth when she is cast off, says your God. For a brief moment I deserted you, but with great compassion I will gather you. In overflowing anger for a moment I hid my face from you, but with everlasting love I will have compassion on you," says the Lord, your Redeemer. "This is like the days of Noah to me: as I swore that the waters of Noah should no more go over the earth, so I have sworn that I will not be angry with you, and will not rebuke you. For the mountains may depart and the hills be removed, but my steadfast love

shall not depart from you, and my covenant of peace shall not be removed," says the Lord, who has compassion on you."No weapon that is fashioned against you shall succeed, and you shall refute every tongue that rises against you in judgment. This is the heritage of the servants of the Lord and their vindication from me, declares the Lord." (Isaiah 54:1, 4-10, 17 ESV)

Caught In the Act

While I was now at a point of weeping at the revelation and the love of God for the broken women, the message did not end there. God reminded me how I had been "caught in the act" so many times before surrendering to His call on my life. He reminded me that I was not alone and that He is seeking those who are "caught" to come home. Again, the next Scripture passage is about a woman being caught in the act of adultery; yet there are many, male and female, who are caught in the trap of sin. This is an invitation for everyone to "go and sin no more, and to return to God."

"The scribes and the Pharisees brought a woman who had been caught in adultery, and placing her in the midst they said to him, 'Teacher, this woman has been caught in the act of adultery. Now in the Law Moses commanded us to stone such women. So what do you say?'"

"And as they continued to ask him, he stood up and said to them, 'Let him who is without sin among you be the first to throw a stone at her.'"

"But when they heard it, they went away one by one, beginning with the older ones, and Jesus was left alone with the woman standing before him. Jesus stood up and said to her, 'Woman, where are they? Has no one condemned you?' She said, 'No one, Lord.' And Jesus

said, 'Neither do I condemn you; go, and from now on sin
no more.' Again Jesus spoke to them, saying, 'I am the
light of the world. Whoever follows me will not walk in darkness, but
will have the light of life.'" (John 8:3-5, 7, 9-12 ESV)

There was yet more:

Living Water—so many are stumbling blindly
through the terrors of our time, perishing of a spiritual thirst.
We need to return to God and show others the way.

"A woman from Samaria came to draw water. Jesus said to her, 'Give
me a drink.' The Samaritan woman said to him, 'How is it that you, a
Jew, ask for a drink from me, a woman of Samaria?' (For Jews have no
dealings with Samaritans.) Jesus answered her, 'If you knew the gift
of God, and who it is that is saying to you, "Give me a drink," you
would have asked him, and he would have given you living water.'
The woman said to him, 'Sir, you have nothing to draw water with,
and the well is deep. Where do you get that living water?'"
(John 4:7-11 ESV)

"Jesus said to her, 'Everyone who drinks of this water will be thirsty
again, but whoever drinks of the water that I will give him will never
be thirsty again. The water that I will give him will become in him a
spring of water welling up to eternal life.' The woman said to him,
"'Sir, give me this water, so that I will not be thirsty or have to come
here to draw water.'"
(John 4:13-15 ESV)

I Have No Husband—with all of the attacks on holy
matrimony these days, there are far too many people who have
neither husband nor wife. America has surely gone astray, with
far too many going each his or her own way; yet the Lord has
laid our sins and iniquity on Jesus. Thank God for the blood.

"Jesus said to her, 'Go, call your husband, and come here.' The woman answered him, 'I have no husband.' Jesus said to her, 'You are right in saying, "I have no husband"; for you have had five husbands, and the one you now have is not your husband. What you have said is true.' The woman said to him, 'Sir, I perceive that you are a prophet.'" (John 4:16-19 ESV)

"Jesus said to her, 'Woman, believe me, the hour is coming when neither on this mountain nor in Jerusalem will you worship the Father. You worship what you do not know; we worship what we know, for salvation is from the Jews. But the hour is coming, and is now here, when the true worshipers will worship the Father in spirit and truth, for the Father is seeking such people to worship him. God is spirit, and those who worship him must worship in spirit and truth.'" (John 4:21-24 ESV)

"So the woman left her water jar and went away into town and said to the people, 'Come, see a man who told me all that I ever did. Can this be the Christ?'" (John 4:28-29 ESV)

Surely now is the time for us [male and female] to "come and see," and to worship our Lord "in spirit and in truth."

For Such a Time as This: The Esther Moment Season

"When Mordecai learned all that had been done, Mordecai tore his clothes and put on sackcloth and ashes, and went out into the midst of the city, and he cried out with a loud and bitter cry."
(Esther 4:1 ESV)

"When Esther's young women and her eunuchs came and told her, the queen was deeply distressed. She sent garments to clothe Mordecai, so that he might take off his sackcloth, but he would not accept them. Then Esther called for Hathach, one of the king's eunuchs, who had been appointed to attend her, and ordered him to

go to Mordecai to learn what this was and why it was."
(Esther 4:4-5 ESV)

"And Mordecai told him all that had happened to him, and the exact sum of money that Haman had promised to pay into the king's treasuries for the destruction of the Jews. Mordecai also gave him a copy of the written decree issued in Susa for their destruction, that he might show it to Esther and explain it to her and command her to go to the king to beg his favor and plead with him on behalf of her people." (Esther 4:7-8 ESV)

"Then Esther spoke to Hathach and commanded him to go to Mordecai and say, 'All the king's servants and the people of the king's provinces know that if any man or woman goes to the king inside the inner court without being called, there is but one law—to be put to death, except the one to whom the king holds out the golden scepter so that he may live. But as for me, I have not been called to come in to the king these thirty days.' And they told Mordecai what Esther had said. Then Mordecai told them to reply to Esther, 'Do not think to yourself that in the king's palace you will escape any more than all the other Jews. For if you keep silent at this time, relief and deliverance will rise for the Jews from another place, but you and your father's house will perish. And who knows whether you have not come to the kingdom for such a time as this?' Then Esther told them to reply to Mordecai, 'Go, gather all the Jews to be found in Susa, and hold a fast on my behalf, and do not eat or drink for three days, night or day. I and my young women will also fast as you do. Then I will go to the king, though it is against the law, and if I perish I perish.' Mordecai then went away and did everything as Esther had ordered him." (Esther 4:10-17 ESV)

America REPENT and Receive Pardon!
An Urgent Notice of the True Meaning of Amnesty

"The Spirit of the Lord is upon me, because he has anointed me to proclaim good news to the poor. He has sent me to proclaim liberty to the captives and recovering of sight to the blind, to set at liberty those who are oppressed." (Luke 4:18 ESV)

Amnesty (from the Greek ἀμνηστία amnestia, "forgetfulness") is defined as: "A pardon extended by the government to a group or class of persons, usually for a political offense; the act of a sovereign power officially forgiving certain classes of persons who are subject to trial but have not yet been convicted."[1] It includes more than pardon, in as much as it obliterates all legal remembrance of the offense. Amnesty is more and more used to express "freedom" and the time when prisoners can go free.

The Trump Factor:

As this book is heading to press, America has elected a new president, Mr. Donald Trump.

Amidst shouts of "we did it" in the victory of Mr. Donald Trump and others elected on November 8, 2016, for some there are tears of frustration that some not so favorite candidates won and their favorites lost in the presidential, Senate, House and gubernatorial bids; yet there is a voice calling from Heaven's courts: "Come together in agape love as the 'One Blood' of Acts 17:26."

"Shout to the Lord, all the earth; break out in praise and sing for joy! Let the hills sing out their songs of joy before the Lord, for he is coming to judge the earth. He will judge

the world with justice and the nations with fairness."
(see Psalm 98)

Let's remember that God has the final say in who ascends to seats of power and who does not. God has decided the outcome. "We the People" have voted in 2016, advancing a shift for the sanctity of life, family and community. The U.S. election is over. Now what?

"Everyone must submit to governing authorities; for
all authority comes from God, and those in positions of
authority have been placed there by God. So anyone
who rebels against authority is rebelling against what God
has instituted, and they will be punished." (Romans 13:1-2 NLT)

For Christians "in spirit and in truth" with what happens moving ahead is our focus. Yesterday is now history.

At the turn of the century, America faced a crossroads. What would the new millennium bring to us? In many ways, for the 21st century's first decade and subsequent years, until election 2016, America was embroiled in civil unrest. Infractions on moral values were strained past a point of endurance. Economic upheaval threatened to topple our economy. Racial tensions mounted. War loomed over our nation, threatening our very existence. That too is now history.

Right now today, it is time to appeal to God for the healing of our nation. Men and women in leadership, and all of the people in this nation and around the world, do not have the power to accomplish this feat alone. Yet: "With God, all things are possible" (Matthew 19:26).

We know that during the 2016 U.S. election cycle, many Christians were praying and fasting even as Queen Esther did for the deliverance of her nation in ancient times. A parallel effect to Esther's and the Christian America's plight is that prayer caused an unprecedented shift in the spirit and God's grace prevailed. Haman dug a ditch and hung on his own gallows.

Time and time again, the Scripture is proven, "The prayer of a righteous person is powerful and effective" (availing much) (James 5:16 NIV).

The charge will always be to remain prayerful and compassionate through times of victory and challenge. The spiritual community must now and always keep praying, listening to, and following and obeying God.

While there are prophecies comparing President-Elect Trump to King Cyrus in the Bible during the days of Daniel, Nehemiah and Ezra, as time passes much more will be revealed.

At the end of the day, no matter what humans say, God has allowed Mr. Trump to rise thus far. However, the proverbial "buck" won't stop with Mr. Trump. We, as Christian believers, must do our part. As America returns to God, we must pray and hold the president accountable.

We must also shoulder our share of the burdens of America. Healing America will require unified acts of faith, hope, love and obedience to God. What happens next is up to God.

"Don't be misled (deceived)—you cannot mock the justice of God. You will always harvest (reap) what you (sow) plant."
(Galatians 6:7 NLT)

As to human politics, we must always remember that no

human men, women or children can save America or the world. Only the God of John 3:16 can do that!

Of one blood, God created the human race
(see Acts 17:26).

We are a human race of ONE BLOOD in need of a Savior.

"For God loved the world so much that he gave his one and only Son, so that everyone who believes in him will not perish but have eternal life." (John 3:16 NLT)

AFTERWORD

Bishop Vincent Matthews, Jr.

In *America Return to God*, Evangelist Alveda King shares a prophetic message for the world. Indeed, we are living in tumultuous times. Alveda King has uncannily given us the cultural context from which we are living, while simultaneously giving us real solutions to lead us out of the abyss. Our world is being manipulated by fear, hate, misunderstanding and arrogance. Alas, one can become hopeless, if looking to mere mortals for relief!

America has been on a collision course because it has a culture of contradiction. While touting freedom in the constitution, our country penned the 3/5th compromise. While supporting intellectualism, the racist, Darwinian theories are touted in our schools and dehumanization and separation of people is normal.

Dr. King has succinctly stated the problem while giving practical solutions.

Hosea 4:6 reminds us, "My people are destroyed for lack of knowledge…" We now know the truth and with this knowledge comes the responsibility to put it into action.

Alveda King astutely demonstrates that Christianity is not about personal comfort, but the Great commission of Christ to reach the world is the answer.

It was illegal for slaves to read and pray! Why? Because knowing brought power. Slaves such as Frederick Douglass, Nat Turner, Henry Highland Garnet, Denmark Vesey, Harriet Tubman, Sojourner Truth, and Toussaint L'Ouverture, all rebelled actively through the knowledge of the Word and their relationship with God. Abolitionists such as John Brown, William Lloyd Garrison and William Wilberforce also allowed the Word of God to transform them.

Just as Alveda King and Matt Lockett reconciled past sins and injustices, we too must allow God to give us a collective Tabula Rasa. If not, the results will continue to be disastrous. We are in danger to follow the mistake of King Jeroboam of Israel, who set a downward spiral for his nation through insecurity and selfishness. We too are in a cyclical decent, but there is hope.

We must think more deeply than the counterproductive forces expect. Those with great power, such as the police, must have a higher level of accountability. The system is flawed, not broken; in fact, it is operating exactly as it was designed. Oppression, fear and control were the intent of elites. Poor whites were used during slavery as mere overseers on plantations and were also the slave catchers (the police of the day) to return freedom-seeking blacks to their degradation. The blacks were slaves and these poor whites had no rights or representation and they could not even vote because they were not land owners. Indeed, the cruel joke today is that we are attempting to fix a system that is inherently corrupt.

We need a new paradigm, a divine way of thinking. Ironically, this fresh thinking comes from a Jewish Rabbi's teachings 2,000 years ago. It is through the radical message and culture of Jesus Christ that we find liberty. It is no wonder that the Reverend Dr. Martin Luther King Jr. mentioned Jesus' teaching in most of his speeches! Consider that Jesus was a minority Jew in the Colonial Roman Empire.

Jesus was born to a poor teenage, single mother in the Middle East. Jesus was not an educated elite. Jesus never went to Europe to the capital of the Empire. Jesus was poor, having never owned a home. Jesus suffered political injustice. Jesus suffered police brutality. Jesus endured biased unjust courts. Jesus was betrayed by His own ethnic group. Jesus was executed by European Colonialists. It seems that Jesus can really relate to this day. Yet, Jesus is the *greatest champion* to ever live, having surmounted all odds and even conquering death!

Evangelist Alveda King has prophetically called us back to the Black Prayer Kettle! We must follow the example of our ancestors and harness the power of Christ to transform the ordinary into the supernatural. Through Christ we can transform our families to empowering places, through Christ we can transform an ordinary child into a life changing citizen, and through Christ we can transform our ordinary communities into life-affirming oases of unity. Through Jesus Christ we can transform our ordinary courts, schools and government into life citadels of true freedom and peace.

Let us embrace the teaching and life of Christ to counter the great evils we face in our communities. The genocide of innocents in American society can be ended if we band together. We must support proper sexual teaching of abstinence, give loving care to the pregnant, adopt the unwanted, and support the downtrodden in our society—just as Jesus Christ teaches us to do.

Indeed, we can repair the gates. This book was a call for all of us to walk in the supernatural and literally change the world! It is possible. Alveda King has reminded us that the fight is not one that is easily won because it is spiritual. Let us conclude with this poignant Scripture from the Holy Bible as a reminder of the fight that we must face, it advises:

"For the weapons of our warfare are not carnal but mighty in God for pulling down strongholds, casting down arguments and every high thing that exalts itself against the knowledge of God, bringing every though into captivity to the obedience of Christ." (2 Corinthians 10:4-5 NKJV)

SELECTED POETRY

All selections by Alveda C. King:

Love's Garden

Whispering softly, love comes into my dreams

Shadow kissed by stardust, dancing with moonbeams.

Robed in promise of eternal delight

The mystery of love unfolding in the night.

Shadow touched by moonlight tender

True love's kiss awakened heart of slumber

King of kings and Lord of lords, the center

Of the love this life proclaims.

For an instant my world trembled

From a touch that came too soon

Steady, heartbeat. Listen. Listen.

For the sun has kissed the moon.

Father, dear, reveal Your plan,

Jesus, You're my life, my joy.

Spirit, tender, Holy, guiding.

Dare I love this mortal man?

You, Lord God, are majestic splendor,

Clothed in excellence divine.

Oh may our love forever please You.

May our will be ever Thine.

Grant to us Your peace, Your power.

Not in our own strength, but Thine.

Make us true and sure and earnest.

Lacking nothing, pure and fine.

You are the Kingdom and the glory.

May Your love be our life story.

And forever we will sing.

Of Your mercy, God, our King!

Politics Can Make You—

Mad

Powerful

Excited

Politics can shape you; Politics can break you

Politics can woo you—to spend and win

Politics can make you. God! Don't let it take you

Body

Soul

Spirit

or politics can make you a political animal.

Voices

You gave life voice

To sing sweet psalms.

Life sings of degradation.

You gave life ears

to hear Your music

Life listens to pagan drums.

Life has many voices, Lord.

We need to only listen.

Of all the voices in my life

Yours is sweetest.

Where Is Passion?

We crave a passion, hot and burning

We long for love, forever yearning

Our flesh deceives us, our loins mislead us

The path of throbbing passion calls us

Where is the joy of love? Nay, lust

Leaves us crawling in the dust

Panting, wanting, needing, pleading

Forever searching, not succeeding.

Until submission, sure and lasting,

Leads us to the source of power

Power, pleasure, joy; Yes, Passion

Wait for us behind the door. When we yield

We know forever, love, yes love,

Forevermore.

Big Momma

It's yo' show, Big Momma.

At least that's what they call you, ain't it?

With yo' minks, and lynx, and diamond studded sphinx,

You strut 'round like some reincarnated Nefertiti.

If someone were to ask you 'bout the Virgin Birth,

(You've given birth befo', but y'ain't no virgin.)

Would you say, "Virgin?" How unfashionable, Virgins

Went out with the bite from that passion fruit, back there,

In the Garden, all those years ago.

Where, in the world,

Can you find a virgin these days?

I sure would like to sink my fangs—

Excuse me—teeth

Into

A Virgin.

Does this turn our mind to blood covenants? Occult violations

Blood spilled out and sucked up over the centuries.

Blood untold, blood washing away the sins of the world?

The covenant blood of the Lamb?

Maybe this is a dream. A fantasy.

A motion picture slice from the mind of a dreamer

Seeking eternity in the arms of Her Savior

Where yo' gonna go?

I don't know

It's yo' show,

Big Momma.

Big Daddy

And what about you,

Big Daddy?

Forgetting wife,

And life,

And family, chasing dreams, making schemes

To out do

Slew

Foot.

Your master plan is to beat the odds

Play the game, make a name

For yourself.

After all, you've grown ain't you?

Old Slew Foot can't possible get one up

On you.

What you got to do

Is to make enough to buy yo' way out

Of that six-foot deep dirt lined condo

Waitin' for you down the way.

Say. . .

The possibility of power; faith shields,

Spirit swords, seems

Ridiculous. Doesn't it?

Like seeking Him while He's findable?

Unrighteous acts can be bindable,

You know?

Anyway, who is He? You can't see Him, or touch

Him.

Although some nuts say they can actually feel Him.

Can't rightly claim to know Him, huh?

But you do know old Slew Foot, don't you?

Lord of rejection, jealousy, murder. . .

Satisfy, gratify, the master of the flesh.

Love, family, joy, peace, must all be sacrificed on

Slew Foot's alter.

Witch's Brew, occultish whispers

Drown out the sound of

Angels wings.

Demonic voices, offer choices,

Porn and lust, and angel dust.

The mark of the beast appears

On the souls

Of our nearest and dearest. . .

Friends?

Be for real! There is a way out,

You know.

His word is food

His word is drink.

His word is power.

The price? Your pride.

Laid aside. Cleansed by the

Blood of the Lamb.

Who is He?

Old Slew Foot knows.

What you gone do?

Big Daddy.

Ripples (In Time and Space)

Libations, fluids rippling on the sands bringing time

and space together—

Bringing souls and spirits together. . .pebbles on the

water, water making ripples,

Ripples in time.

"Behold I shew you a mystery; We shall not all sleep,

but we shall all be changed

In a moment, in the twinkling of an eye, at the last

Trump; For the trumpet shall sound, and the dead

shall be raised

Incorruptible

And we shall be changed."

Libations, shadows rippling on the sand

The earth beneath my feet changes from my dark

and musky Mother, becoming red and alien, harsh,

As the waters ripple and the great ship rolls.

I am carried away from my familiar jungle of fruits

and passion flowers, wild

Animal friends and even wilder beasts;

Four-legged animals, predators and yet, magnificent

creations of God, with

Skins and furs. . . and fangs.

Yet, change carries us over waters

that no longer Ripple

The water becomes an awesome, rolling jungle of waves

That carry us on in the Middle Passage

Washing us away from our home ground to a new land

of tears and sorrow,

Our newfound home in a new world.

And yet, wherever we were bought,

Beaten and scattered, over continents and islands,

New blood was added to our veins; and yet the Blood of our

Motherland remained,

True and deep.

In our new world, we learned to harvest new crops;

Some not quite so different from our jungle fruits and

vegetation.

We tamed fields of cotton and tobacco

Even as our wild, free spirits were tamed by the new predator;

Two-legged beasts, still creatures of God, and not quite so

magnificent in their

Borrowed skins and furs.

But still their fangs, though changed

Remain deadly.

The libations continue

The spirits that were summoned bring new birth to memories

Reflections of time itself.

We see ourselves in a new jungle still a part of God's creation,

And yet, the earth has changed.

The soil is not dark and musty between our bare

and braceleted feet,

Nor is it red and cracked beneath our chained and callous feet.

It has become rock, concrete,

A machine-made improvement on nature,

And yet still part of nature.

The tribal dancers before the sun, the wind,

the rain and the moon

Have become whirling disco bodies beneath

a myriad of simulated starlight,

Lightning and thundering electrophonic sounds.

The hunter's spears and darts have become a mania for money;

And guns bring down men and prey upon the weak who are

homeless, jobless, and dreamless.

The savagery continues, though times and methods change.

Humankind has changed, and yet has not changed, only

Shimmered and rippled in the reflections of time.

For though one generation passeth away, another generation

Cometh. As the sun rises, it sets only to rise again.

The wind goes to the south only to return to the north,

Whirling continually, returning again according to its

Circuits. And the rivers run to the sea, yet the sea is not full,

For the rivers return again to that place from which they came.

For that which has been, shall be again, and that which has

been done,

Shall be done again.

For as all things change, they remain because: "There is no new

thing under the sun."

There are only

Rippling images of change, all belonging to the universe, the

Old, the New

Created by the Omnipotent

The Lord God! Who changes not.

For Generations to Come

Our family tree

Means more to me,

Than silver or gold, or a

Rolls Royce.

I can rejoice and be glad,

That mother and dad loved each other —

and God

Who blessed their union.

From one to another, we are linked

To each other...

Through the blessings and mercy or our awesome

Creator

Our Creator, the Artist, Who reminds us of

Eternity

In the smiles of our children, who have the

Spirit of our ancestors —

Twinkling out from their eyes . . .

Reminding us

Of

Generations to come.

SJ Forevermore

SJ, today

You lift me up.

Yesterday, you filled my cup.

Tomorrow and forevermore,

You are my keys to Heaven's door.

Praise to

Father

Son

And Spirit.

Thanks, SJ,

Forever.

P.S. thanks for breaking bonds and curses.

Sunshine feels real good.

Beloved,

Is the moon ashamed of the glory of the sun?

Is the believer ashamed of the Gospel of Jesus Christ?

I count it an honor and a privilege to know you and be a part of
your life.

Your strength, your wisdom, the beauty of your spirit are like
spring rain to my soul.

Forgive the frailties of my human spirit. The iniquities that
plague my DNA if you will.

Love, eternal love that is, overcomes obstacles.

You are my heart's desire, and I expect

That God will move mightily in our lives.

May God's strength be yours, His will your

will. My prayers and my love are with you always,

even before the foundations of the

world, we truly were in God's plan. I love you.

Never forget or doubt for a single second, that I love you, even

as I love our heavenly

Father, who has ordained that we would meet and love and

encourage each other.

I await all things in joy, anticipation, and patience.

A Creation Parable

I emerged from the womb of an ancient goddess, known by many as Eve. Her husband Adam was also a god favored by the Almighty Creator. Adam and Eve were the first power couple known to humankind. Adam walked with Great Creator I AM in the Garden of the great country of Eden during the cool of the day.

Adam's intellect was so superior that he was able to name all the plants and animals that inhabited Adam's palatial mansion, called Earth. Mother or Planet Earth was uniquely beautiful in those days. The climate and atmosphere were perfect, ripe for procreative abundance. Great Creator I AM was so pleased with all that Great Creator I AM had made, that Great Creator I AM gave Adam and Eve full license to "be fruitful and multiply."

Indeed, Adam's physical body had been formed from the substance of Mother Earth. Great Creator I AM fashioned Adam's magnificent body from the dust of Mother Earth. Later, Great Creator I AM caused mighty Adam to fall into a deep sleep. Then, Great Creator I AM took DNA and RNA substance from Adam and fashioned our ancient, beautiful and powerful goddess Mother Eve.

For many years, Adam and Eve resided primarily in the Garden of Eden on their planet. Together they had dominion over everything. Then, one day, an adversary of the Creator, who had been banished from the Royal Courts of Great Creator I AM made his evil advance into the Paradise of Adam and Eve.

This particularly cunning enemy was very jealous of Adam and Eve, because, having rebelled against the Mighty Great Creator I AM, the adversary Lucifer lost his lofty authority in the heavens. Lucifer had been foolish enough to say that he would exalt himself above the heavenly throne of Great Creator I AM. Needless to explain, but I will attempt it anyway, Great Creator I AM was not about to be dethroned, so Lucifer and his companions, in the crime of treason against Great Creator I AM, were cast out of the heavens into outer darkness.

Then, one day, the Holy Spirit of Great Creator I AM moved over the interplanetary shadows of a heretofore unnoticed planet called Earth. Great Creator I AM spoke energy light into the atmosphere of Mother Earth, and life appeared on the planet. This is where Great Creator I AM fashioned Adam and Eve and established their Earthly Kingdom in the Garden of Eden.

Enemy Lucifer would not leave well enough alone. He hated his exile. After all, he had been the choir leader in Heaven. He was the most talented and the most beautiful of all the angels. His elevated status had never been enough. He "wanted it all." Never has there been a greater example of self-love, than that of Lucifer.

The banishment of the fallen angel Lucifer/Satan is noted as being so severe that the only begotten Son of Great Creator I AM would one day recall that He saw this ancient serpentine enemy fall from planet Heaven like lightening.

At any rate, Angel Lucifer, as he was known at the time, decided to slither into the Garden of Eden and seduce Adam's wife. His seduction was so effective that it disrupted the harmony of Eden.

Enemy Lucifer wanted Earth but had no legal way to wrest it from Adam. So, Lucifer seduced Mother Eve. Mother Eve tried to reason out in her own mind the edicts of Great Creator I AM that had been given to her husband Adam. They were not to eat of the knowledge of the tree of good and evil. Eve was beguiled by Lucifer and ate of the fruit. Adam was not beguiled, but a part of himself, his DNA/RNA connection to Eve had already partaken, so he joined his wife in the act of partaking of the "forbidden fruit."

After the fruit of forbidden knowledge was conceived, Great Creator I AM cast them out of the Garden, away from the tree of life. Adam and Eve, whose spiritual energy and perfectly balanced souls had been housed in a perfect physical body, were now subject to time. They moved out of the timeless dimensions of Eden, into the boundaries of time and decay of what earth would become.

Great Creator I AM placed a flaming sword at the "gate" of Eden so that Adam and Eve would not have the courage to "walk through the fire" to return to Paradise.

In the midst of Lucifer's seduction and Adam and Eve's subsequent "fall from Great Creator I AM's grace," two sons were conceived; Cain being of his father the evil one, and Able being the Son of Adam. Cain, in a fit of rage, killed Abel. Murder was now in the earth.

Adam's and Eve's bodies, no longer eternally existing in a timeless state, began to "die." Great Creator I AM had warned them that not following the Creator's divine instructions would lead to "death." This state of "death" had previously been unknown to creation.

Over the next thousands of years, men and women would be born, and then die on Planet Earth. Only the promise of a "Redeemer" gave the people hope.

Great Creator I AM had a timeless plan. "For Great Creator I AM so loved the world, that Great Creator I AM gave Great Creator I AM's only begotten Son, Jesus, so that anyone who believes on, has faith in and accepts the Lordship of Jesus the Christ, shall not perish, but shall have the everlasting life promised to us before the beginning of time as we know and understand it."

Much of this truth has been distorted by human reasoning and demonic interference. Yet, Great Creator I AM loves us so much that we are welcome into eternity if we accept the Way, the Truth and the Life.

Pursue Truth, and Life. Amen.

John 1:1, "In the beginning was the Word, and the Word was with God and the Word was God."

END NOTES

All definitions referenced are from www.dictionary.com and www.bing.com.

Chapter 1.

[1] http://www.religioustolerance.org/chr_prac.htm. This is a reduction from 55% in 1991. Attendance data are grossly inflated. Independent studies that count actual participation have revealed that the actual attendance values are typically one-half of those found by polls. People tend to respond to pollsters according to how they feel they should act, or according to how they feel society expects them to act, not according to how actually they do act.

[2] http://www.dictionary.com

Chapter 2.

[1] https://en.wikipedia.org/wiki/September_11_attacks
[2] https://en.wikipedia.org/wiki/World_Trade_Center_site

Chapter 3.

[1] http://muncherian.com/s-mal3v7.html
[2] http://www.crosswalk.com/church/worship/churchianity-revealed-11549412.html?ps=0

Chapter 4.

[1] http://www.timwise.org/tag/white-privilege
[2] http://elijahlist.com/words/display_word.html?ID=16176

Chapter 5.

[1] http://www.raystedman.org/bible-overview/adventuring/nehemiah-rebuilding-the-walls

Chapter 9.

[1] http://www.hiddenmeanings.com/Sermon35eunuchs.htm
[2] http://www.charismamag.com/life/women/23725-when-linda-confessed-her-lesbianism-to-her-pastor
[3] Scripture references regarding sexual sins including but not limited to homosexuality and other forms of perversion such as rape, pornography, masturbation, and other issues: Genesis 19:1-13, Leviticus 18:21-22 and 20:13, Judges 19:22, Romans 1:26-27, Galatians 5:19.

Additional research links:
I shared my views on why "Gay Marriage is Impossible" at a summit at Family Research Council in Washington, D.C. with Honorable Ken Blackwell of Family Research Council and Deacon Keith Fournier of the Catholic Online: https://youtu/WMvSz2xsAik.

http://thestarofzion.com/board-of-bishops-issue-official-statement-regarding-supreme-court-ruling-on-p586-1.htm
http://www.priestsforlife.org/library/5154-and-it-all-started-with-an-apple

http://www.catholic.org/news/national/story.php?id=61767
http://mobile.wnd.com/2015/06/civil-rights-leader-speaks-out-on-marriage-ruling/#YC91xxOI5hpsiuGh.99
[4] Some of the ideologies in "one-flesh bond" are also from Dr. James Robertson

Chapter 10:

[1] https://en.m.wikipedia.org/wiki/Amnesty#cite_note-1

Thank You

To God be all the glory!

To my family, God bless you.

To my church family, God bless you too!

To my friends and peers in my circle of influence

and dominion territory,

God bless you as we continue to be victorious

on the battlefield of life.

To my publicists, publishers, and editors, God bless you!

Thank you ladies and gentlemen for reading this book,

for spending time with me this way.

Thanks also for your testimonies.

God has planted His purpose in every one of us.

May yours be fulfilled

to the greatest extent as your gifts, talents and

callings are increasingly released for His Glory!

Share this message everywhere you go:

"For God so loved the world, that He gave

His only begotten Son,

that whosoever believes on Him shall not perish,

but shall have Everlasting life." (John 3:16)

May God Bless You richly,

Evangelist Alveda C. King

ABOUT THE AUTHOR AND RESOURCES

Evangelist Alveda C. King works toward her purpose in life, to glorify God.

Alveda C. King is a Christian evangelist and civil rights activist and is also known for her creative contributions in film, music and journalism. She is also an actress, singer, songwriter, blogger, author and a television and radio personality. As a former GA State Legislator, Director of Civil Rights for the Unborn for Priests for Life, and devoted mother and grandmother, she is also a guardian of the King Family Legacy. Alveda is the daughter of Rev. A. D. King and Mrs. Naomi King, the granddaughter of Rev. Martin Luther King, Sr. and Mrs. Alberta Williams King, and the niece of Dr. Martin Luther King, Jr.

Alveda King grew up in the civil rights movement led by her uncle, Dr. Martin Luther King, Jr. Her family home in Birmingham, Alabama, was bombed, as was her father's church office in Louisville, Kentucky. Alveda was jailed during the open housing movement. She sees the pro-life movement as a continuation of the civil rights struggle.

Evangelist King is a former college professor and served in the Georgia State House of Representatives. She is a recipient of the Life Prize Award (2011), the Cardinal John O'Connor Pro-Life Hall of Fame Award (2011) from the Legatus organization and the Civil Rights Award from Congress of Racial Equality (CORE) (2011). She is a bestselling author; among her books are *King Rules: Ten Truths for You, Your Family, and Our Nation to Prosper, How Can the Dream Survive if we Murder the Children? and I Don't Want Your Man, I Want My Own.* She is an accomplished actress and songwriter. The Founder of Alveda King Ministries, Alveda is also the recipient of an honorary Doctorate of Laws degree from Saint Anselm College. Alveda is a regular columnist for Newsmax.com "Insiders" section and a *Fox News* contributor.

Evangelist King lives in Atlanta, where she is the grateful mother of six and a doting grandmother.

Websites: www.alvedaking.com
www.priestsforlife.org

Mailing Address: ALVEDA KING MINISTRIES
3645 Marketplace Blvd. Ste. 130-592
East Point., GA., USA 30344

Elijah List Publications Resources:

THE ELIJAH LIST: www.elijahlist.com

Prophetic TV: www.prophetic.tv
ELIJAH LIST Ministries: www.elijahlistministries.com
ELIJAH SHOPPER: www.elijahshopper.com
Amazing Health Advances: www.amazinghealthadvances.com
Breaking Christian News: www.breakingchristiannews.com

Additional copies of this book and other products from
Elijah List Publications are available at our Elijah Shopper
store at www.elijahshopper.com.

Call toll-free: 1-866-354-5245 or 1-541-926-3250

ELIJAH LIST PUBLICATIONS

*"The lion has roared—who will not fear? The Sovereign
LORD has spoken—who can but prophesy?" —Amos 3:8*

Elijah List Publications
528 Ellsworth St. SW Albany, OR 97321

Visit us at www.elijahlist.com